USA TODAY

USA TODAY'S DEBATE: VOICES AND PERSPECTIVES

# DEATH PENALTY

## Fair Solution or Moral Failure?

JoAnn Bren Guernsey

TFCB

Twenty-First Century Books · Minneapolis

Twenty-First Century Books
A division of Lerner Publishing Group, Inc.
241 First Avenue North
Minneapolis, MN 55401 U.S.A.

Website address: www.lernerbooks.com

The publisher wishes to thank Ben Nussbaum and Phil Pruitt of USA TODAY for their help in preparing this book.

Library of Congress Cataloging-in-Publication Data

Guernsey, JoAnn Bren.
Death Penalty: Fair Solution or Moral Failure? / by JoAnn Bren Guernsey.
p. cm. — (USA today's debate: voices and perspectives)
Includes bibliographical references and index.
ISBN: 978-0-7613-4079-9 (lib. bdg. : alk. paper)
1. Death penalty. I. Title.
HV8694.G83 2010
364.66—dc22 2006028984

Manufactured in the United States of America
1 2 3 4 5 6 - DP - 15 14 13 12 11 10

# CONTENTS

"America's youth need to read this book." —Judy Briscoe,
Director of Delinquency Prevention, Texas Youth Commission
LIFE IN PRISON
STOP
STATE
SAVE
STAN!
SAVE STAN TOOKIE WILLIAMS
STOP THE RACIST DEATH PENALTY

# Introduction

ON THE NIGHT OF DECEMBER 12, 2005, MORE than two thousand demonstrators gathered outside the gates of San Quentin State Prison near San Francisco, California. They had come to express support for Stanley "Tookie" Williams. Williams was a convicted murderer and founder of the Crips, a street gang based in Los Angeles, California. Many years before, the state of California had sentenced Williams, an African American man, to death for his crimes. His legal team had fought to change the sentence, but their efforts over the years had been unsuccessful.

Outside, the demonstrators lit candles and sang hymns. Some waved signs reading "Save Tookie" and "Abolish the Racist Death Penalty." Several well-known speakers, including civil rights leader Jesse Jackson and folksinger Joan Baez, addressed the crowd. They and many others had fought hard to save Williams's life. But their efforts had also failed. Williams was scheduled to be executed, or put to death, at midnight.

Dozens of reporters and photographers attended the rally. A few counterdemonstrators came to the rally

*Left:* Demonstrators gather outside the gates of San Quentin State Prison in California on the eve of the execution of Stanley "Tookie" Williams in 2005.

too. One held a picture of Yee-Chen Lin, her face turned into a bloody mess by a shotgun blast. Almost twenty-five years earlier, Williams had been convicted of murdering her and three others during two separate robberies. The counterdemonstrators felt that Williams's death sentence was just. They believed he deserved to die for the murders of four innocent people.

But Williams's supporters argued that he was a changed man. During his years in prison, Williams had renounced violence. He had cowritten a series of children's books, designed to steer young people away from gangs and drugs. In 2004 he had negotiated a truce between the Crips and a rival street gang, the Bloods. Williams had won supporters around the world. He had even been nominated for a Nobel Peace Prize.

At midnight, as the crowd outside sang and spoke in the chilly December air, prison staff gave Williams a lethal injection. This shot of three different drugs knocked Williams unconscious, paralyzed him and stopped his breathing, and then stopped his heart. He was pronounced dead shortly after midnight.

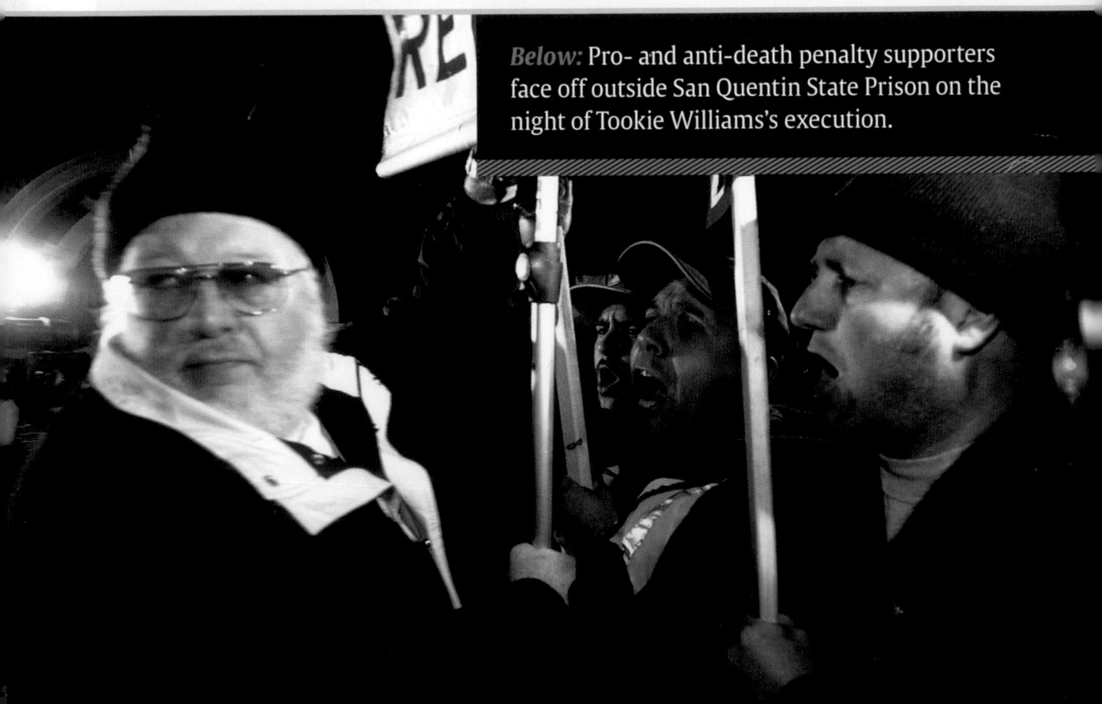

*Below:* Pro- and anti-death penalty supporters face off outside San Quentin State Prison on the night of Tookie Williams's execution.

Had justice been served? Lora Owens, whose stepson Albert had been one of Williams's victims, felt that it had. She had fought hard to see the death sentence carried out. In November 2005, she had written to California governor Arnold Schwarzenegger, asking him to deny a last-minute request to stop the execution. Owens told the governor: Williams "is not a model citizen" as some had claimed. "He is a murderer and has caused the Owens family anguish for the last 26 years."

But Williams's supporters argued that nothing had been gained by killing him. They denounced the execution, which Baez described as "planned, efficient, calculated, antiseptic, cold-blooded murder." They pointed out the many flaws in the U.S. death penalty system. They said the system is biased against African Americans and poor people. They said that killing anyone—even a convicted murderer—is wrong.

The Tookie Williams case gained worldwide attention. It highlighted many of the debates and questions that swirl around the death penalty (also called capital punishment): Is the death penalty just? Is it cruel and inhumane? Does the threat of the death penalty keep people from committing murder? Does the death penalty system discriminate against African Americans and other minorities? What if the government executed an innocent person by mistake? Should a mentally ill person be executed? What about a person like Williams, who became a better man in prison?

The answers to these questions vary, depending on whom you ask. Victims' families, lawyers, judges, politicians, and everyday citizens all have different views. Some groups want to outlaw the death penalty. Other groups favor its use. Both sides use websites, books, statistics, and studies to win supporters, influence public opinion, and change laws. Arguments between the two groups often grow heated. The following chapters examine these debates more closely.

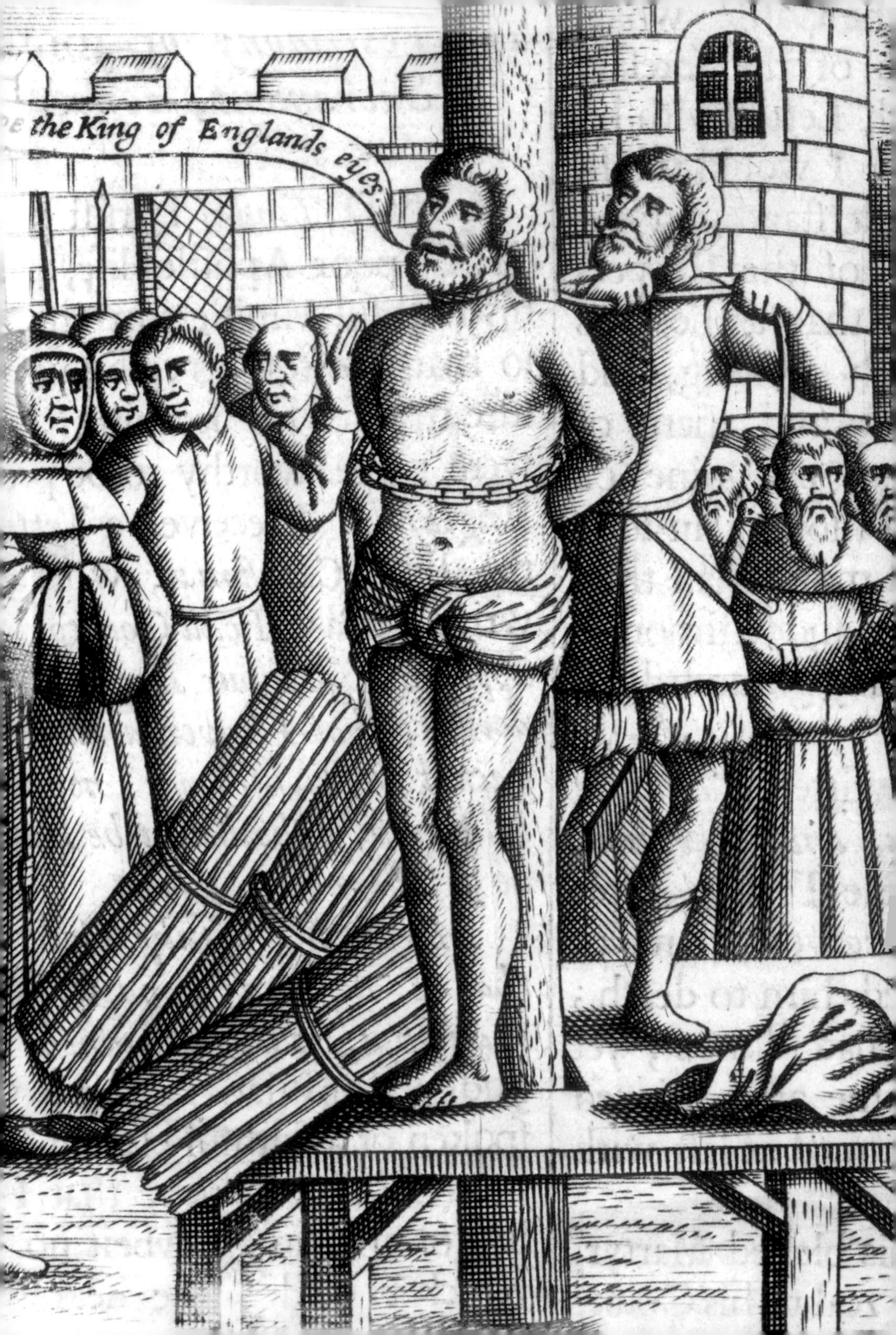

e the King of Englands eyes.

## CHAPTER ONE

# Execution through the Ages

CAPITAL PUNISHMENT—PUNISHMENT BY DEATH—is an old idea. The Code of Hammurabi, a legal document from ancient Babylonia (in modern-day Iraq), contained the first known death penalty laws. Under the code, written in the 1700s B.C., twenty-five crimes were punishable by death. These crimes included adultery (cheating on a wife or husband) and helping slaves escape. Murder was not one of the twenty-five crimes.

The Hebrew Bible, a collection of writings from ancient Israel, also set down rules of law. According to the Bible, an offender should give "life for life, eye for eye, tooth for tooth, hand for hand, foot for foot." In other words, "the punishment should fit the crime." In this philosophy, someone who takes a life should pay with his or her own life.

The Hittites, Greeks, Romans, Egyptians, and other ancient groups also imposed the death penalty for certain crimes. Methods of execution were usually brutal. They included beheading, drowning, burning, and stoning.

During the Middle Ages (about A.D. 500 to 1500), many societies continued to practice capital punishment. Condemned people might be burned at the stake, hanged,

*Left:* This drawing, based on a sixteenth-century English woodcut, shows a man being executed for his crimes by the local authorities.

beheaded, pressed under heavy weights, or boiled to death. Executions took place in public and usually attracted big crowds, eager to see criminals put to death. Afterward, executioners often put the dead bodies on display as a warning to would-be wrongdoers.

In England in the 1600s, more than one hundred crimes were punishable by death. These crimes included murder, theft, arson (intentionally burning property), cutting down someone else's trees, and stealing rabbits. The English government sometimes executed children for such crimes.

When English colonists came to America, starting in the 1600s, they brought the death penalty with them. Laws varied from colony to colony. In some colonies, people could be executed for murder, adultery, witchcraft, robbery, rape, and arson. In 1608 Captain George Kendall was the first person executed in the American colonies. His crime was working as a spy for Spain, an enemy of England at the time.

The English, meanwhile, found their prisons overflowing in the early 1600s. The authorities sometimes gave condemned prisoners a choice—execution or transportation to the Americas to work as unpaid servants for a term of seven or fourteen years. Most prisoners chose the second option. The British Transportation Act of 1718 standardized the transportation system. For the next fifty years, ships carried thousands of British criminals to North America. Most of them served their terms and became law-abiding colonial citizens, but some of them reverted to their criminal ways.

## NEW VOICES

During the 1700s, a few writers and philosophers began to question whether the death penalty was just and ethical. In 1767 Cesare Beccaria, an Italian scholar, wrote *An Essay on Crimes and Punishments.* In it, he argued that capital punishment was barbaric. He believed that killing criminals made a nation more brutal.

"Is it not absurd," he added, "that the laws, which detest and punish homicide [murder], should, in order to prevent murder, publicly commit murder themselves?" Beccaria also noted that the threat of capital punishment was unlikely to deter, or prevent, anyone from committing murder in the future.

*Above:* Cesare Beccaria was an Italian scholar who argued against the death penalty in the late 1700s.

Back in North America, the United States became a new nation in 1783. Within the nation, death penalty laws varied from state to state. Most state and federal leaders supported the death penalty. But some leaders wanted to see the penalty applied more sparingly. In the early 1800s, some U.S. states passed laws that limited capital punishment to crimes such as murder and treason (betraying one's country). In 1834 Pennsylvania passed a law banning public executions. In 1852 and 1853, respectively, Rhode Island and Wisconsin abolished the death penalty altogether (Rhode Island later reinstated the death penalty).

## MORE HUMANE?

During the nineteenth century, hanging and firing squads were the most common methods of execution in the United States. These punishments were violent and painful. During hangings, the condemned person didn't always die instantly but sometimes choked to death slowly. Death by firing squad was quick but bloody. Reformers searched for more efficient and humane methods of execution.

In the 1880s, inventor Thomas Edison started building electrical lighting systems in U.S. cities. Edison's company demonstrated the power of electricity by electrocuting animals (killing them with electricity). These demonstrations led some people to reason that electrocution was a quick and painless form of execution.

On August 6, 1890, New York State used an "electric chair" to carry out the first execution by electrocution. The condemned was murderer William Kemmler. As it turned out, the process was hardly quick or painless. It took two surges of electricity, one of them lasting more than one minute, to kill Kemmler. The electricity burned Kemmler to death. Despite the gruesome procedure, people still thought electrocution was more humane and efficient than previous methods. With some refinements, it soon became the preferred method of execution in the United States.

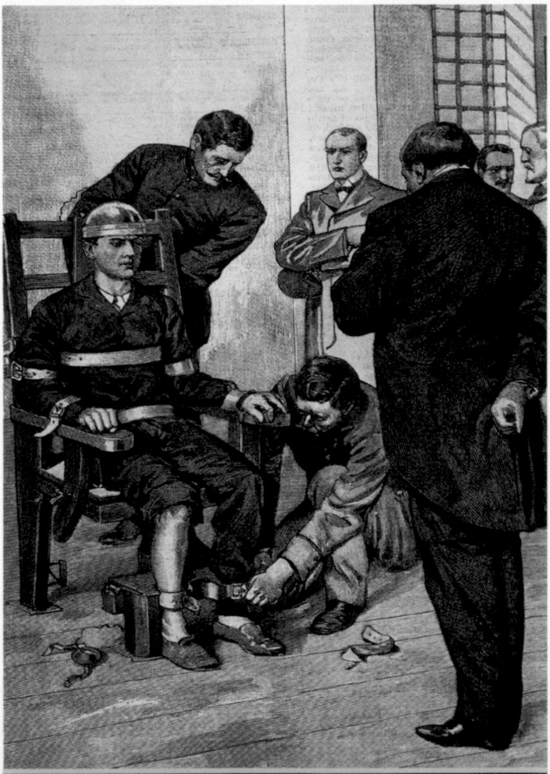

*Above:* Leon Czolgosz, the assassin of U.S. president William McKinley, was executed by electrocution in 1901.

Another new method of execution at the time was gassing. In this procedure, the condemned person sits in a sealed room, strapped

## Capital Crimes

Crimes punishable by death are called capital crimes. Murder is the only capital crime in most death penalty states. A few states also apply the death penalty for treason and aircraft hijacking, and for drug trafficking and kidnapping that result in death.

Until 2008 child rape was a capital crime in six U.S. states. In June 2008, the U.S. Supreme Court heard the case of a man convicted of raping his eight-year-old stepdaughter in Louisiana. The Louisiana court had sentenced the man to death, but the Supreme Court ruled that "the death penalty is not a proportional [appropriate] punishment for the rape of a child." This ruling overturned all state laws making child rape a capital crime.

to a chair. Executioners then release a deadly gas into the room, killing the condemned person within minutes. The first U.S. execution by gas took place in Nevada in 1924. But gassing wasn't quick or painless either. Witnesses often described condemned people moaning, thrashing about, and struggling for breath before finally dying.

### THE SUPREME COURT WEIGHS IN

Most Americans supported the death penalty, and executions continued at a steady pace in the 1930s and 1940s. The all-time high point for U.S. executions occurred in 1935, when U.S. states executed a total of 197 people.

In the 1950s and 1960s—a period of social reform movements—some Americans began to call for an end to capital punishment. Groups such as the American Civil Liberties Union (ACLU) and the National Association for the Advancement of Colored People (NAACP) charged that the death penalty was applied unfairly. For instance, in the U.S. South, black men who raped white women usually received death sentences. Yet white men who raped black women usually went unpunished.

Many European nations either abolished or limited capital punishment during the mid-twentieth century. Some U.S. states also abolished capital punishment during these years. By 1966 support for capital punishment had reached an all-time low in the United States. A poll revealed that only 42 percent of Americans supported the death penalty.

Also during this era, many inmates began challenging their death sentences in state and federal courts. The court cases opened up many new questions about capital punishment. In a series of cases, the U.S. Supreme Court considered whether capital punishment violated the U.S. Constitution. In 1967, while awaiting the Supreme Court ruling, all states stopped executing prisoners.

In 1972, in the case of *Furman v. Georgia*, the Supreme Court ruled that the death penalty amounted to "cruel and unusual punishment," which meant it violated the Eighth Amendment to the U.S. Constitution. The Court also said the death penalty was applied in arbitrary and capricious ways—that is, unevenly and inconsistently. Thus, the Court decreed, the death penalty denied Americans equal protection of the law as described in the Fourteenth Amendment. The Court's decision did not abolish the death penalty, however. The Court

> **"Why are we that concerned about whether a convicted murderer feels some pain at death? It's supposed to be punishment."**
>
> —**KENT SCHEIDEGGER,** CRIMINAL JUSTICE LEGAL FOUNDATION, 2006
>
> **USA TODAY · DECEMBER 18, 2006**

> **"My impression is that lethal injection as practiced in the U.S. now is no more humane than the gas chamber or electrocution, which have both been deemed inhumane."**
>
> —LEONIDAS KONIARIS,
> SURGEON WHO CONDUCTED RESEARCH ON LETHAL INJECTION, 2005

said that capital punishment could continue if states improved their laws to ensure that the penalty was applied more fairly and consistently.

### EXECUTIONS RESUME

Many states did change their laws—writing new ones in anticipation of an eventual Supreme Court ruling that would again allow capital punishment. That ruling came in 1976, when the Court reversed its earlier decision on cruel and unusual punishment. In *Gregg v. Georgia*, the Court stated that "the infliction of death as a punishment for murder is not without justification and . . . is not unconstitutionally severe."

This ruling opened the way for electrocutions, gassings, and other kinds of executions to resume in the United States. In 1977 Gary Gilmore, a Utah murderer, became the first convict executed in the nation in ten years. Gilmore was killed by a firing squad.

Also in 1977, scientists invented lethal injection. Like electrocution and gassing, this new method of execution was thought to kill people quickly and painlessly. In 1982 Texas's Charlie Brooks (convicted of murder) became the first person in the world to be executed by lethal injection.

### COMPLEX QUESTIONS

Throughout the 1980s and 1990s, the Supreme Court continued to grapple with capital punishment cases. It considered whether death sentences

*Above:* This scene from *Dead Man Walking* shows Sister Helen Prejean, played by Susan Sarandon *(left)*, sitting in a courtroom in support of death row inmate Matthew Poncelet (based on Patrick Sonnier,) played by Sean Penn *(right)*.

were racially biased, whether mentally ill people should be executed, whether people should be executed for crimes they committed as teenagers, and other complex questions. State courts considered similar issues. Among the American public, support for the death penalty increased. By the mid-1990s, polls showed that 80 percent of Americans supported capital punishment.

But the anti–death penalty movement was also strong. Abolitionists such as Sister Helen Prejean, a Catholic nun, fought to end capital punishment. A 1996 Hollywood movie, *Dead Man Walking*, dramatized Prejean's friendship with an inmate who had been sentenced to death. The film also awakened the public to the complexities of the death penalty controversy.

Meanwhile, the death penalty system moved ahead. Timothy McVeigh, convicted of killing 168 people in a bombing in Oklahoma City, Oklahoma, was sentenced to death in 1997. One year later, murderer Karla Faye Tucker was executed in Texas.

# Challenge to Lethal Injection

Lethal injection is the most common form of execution in the United States. Since its development in the late 1970s, the three-drug injection has been called a humane method of execution. But in recent years, some medical experts have challenged that claim. They charge that the drug used to knock an inmate unconscious during execution can wear off too soon. If that happens, the inmate will undergo extreme pain and suffering when the second drug (which paralyzes the inmate and stops his or her breathing) and the third drug (which stops the heart) take effect.

In addition, many doctors and nurses refuse to administer lethal injections because killing people violates their professional mission to save, not end, life. For that reason, many prisons rely on less skilled medical technicians to administer lethal injections. Observers note that technicians are more likely than doctors or nurses to mix up the drugs or administer them in incorrect dosages.

In the early 2000s, several inmates appealed their death sentences, charging that lethal injection was cruel and unusual punishment. In September 2007, one of the cases, *Baze v. Rees*, reached the Supreme Court. At that point, states with the death penalty put their executions on hold, awaiting the Court's decision. In April 2008, the Court ruled: "Simply because an execution method may result in pain does not establish the sort of objectively intolerable risk of harm that qualifies as cruel and unusual." Once the ruling was announced, states resumed executions. States also reviewed their procedures to improve lethal injection methods.

The Tucker case attracted worldwide attention. Supporters, including Pope John Paul II, noted that Tucker had become a thoughtful and religious woman during her years in prison. They asked Texas governor George W. Bush to spare her life. But Bush, who later became U.S. president, let the execution go forward. Tucker became the first woman executed in Texas since the Civil War (1861–1865).

The high point for executions in the modern era was 1999, when ninety-eight convicts were put to death in the United States. At the same time, death penalty opponents kept working to stop executions. In 1999 the *Chicago Tribune* published a series of articles showing that people involved in the Illinois justice system—police officers, lawyers, judges, juries, and witnesses—sometimes made mistakes and sometimes treated suspects and criminals unfairly. In a few cases, police even beat suspects to make them confess to crimes they hadn't committted. The articles claimed that innocent people sometimes ended up in Illinois prisons—even with death sentences.

The articles alarmed Illinois governor George Ryan. He worried that if the system weren't fixed, an innocent person might someday be put to death in Illinois. Rather than take that chance, in 2000 Ryan declared a moratorium, or temporary suspension, on executions in his state. In 2003 he commuted (reduced) the sentences of 167 Illinois inmates from death to life in prison. Death penalty opponents praised Ryan's move. Others, especially family members of murder victims, denounced his decision.

## CRIME AND PUNISHMENT

In the early 2000s, executions continued and brutal murders continued. After six years of legal proceedings, Timothy McVeigh died by lethal injection in June 2001. In November 2003, John Allen Muhammad and Lee Boyd Malvo went on a random shooting spree in the Washington, D.C., area. In three weeks, the two men killed ten people and wounded three others. The

## Executions in the United States 1977–2008

Number of Executions Each Year

| | | | |
|---|---|---|---|
| 1977 | 1 | 1993 | 38 |
| 1978 | 0 | 1994 | 31 |
| 1979 | 2 | 1995 | 56 |
| 1980 | 0 | 1996 | 45 |
| 1981 | 1 | 1997 | 74 |
| 1982 | 2 | 1998 | 68 |
| 1983 | 5 | 1999 | 98 |
| 1984 | 21 | 2000 | 85 |
| 1985 | 18 | 2001 | 66 |
| 1986 | 18 | 2002 | 71 |
| 1987 | 25 | 2003 | 65 |
| 1988 | 11 | 2004 | 59 |
| 1989 | 16 | 2005 | 60 |
| 1990 | 23 | 2006 | 53 |
| 1991 | 14 | 2007 | 42 |
| 1992 | 31 | 2008 | 37 |

state of Virginia sentenced Muhammad to death for his crimes. Malvo, who was only seventeen at the time of the shootings, received life in prison. In 2005 murderer Kenneth Lee Boyd became the one thousandth person executed in the United States since capital punishment resumed in 1977.

In September 2007, states again put executions on hold while awaiting a Supreme Court ruling. The case before the Court involved lethal injection, by then the primary method of execution in the United States. Death penalty opponents argued before the Court that lethal injection, if administered incorrectly, causes excruciating pain and is therefore cruel and unusual punishment. In April 2008, the Court ruled in *Baze v. Rees* that lethal injection is not cruel and unusual, and executions resumed. At that point, more than 3,300 U.S. inmates were awaiting execution.

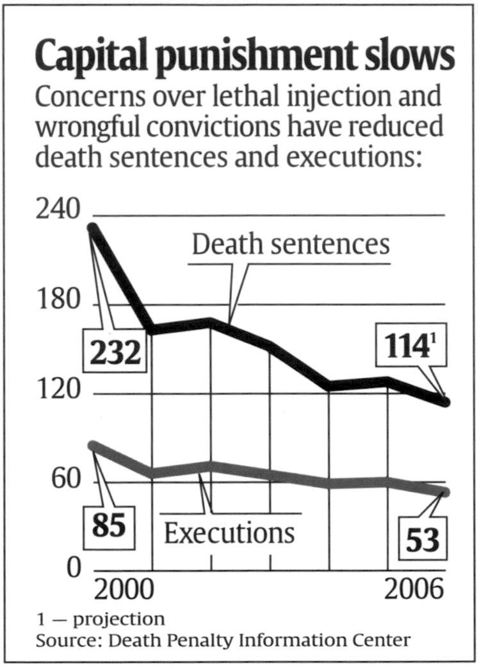


**Capital punishment slows**

Concerns over lethal injection and wrongful convictions have reduced death sentences and executions:

1 — projection

Source: Death Penalty Information Center

By Robert W. Ahrens, USA TODAY, 2006

USA TODAY News SECTION A

April 17, 2008

# High court clears way to restart lethal injections

From the Pages of USA TODAY

WASHINGTON—Several states are poised to resume executions after the Supreme Court on Wednesday upheld Kentucky's lethal injection method and effectively ended a national moratorium.

The Court majority rejected arguments that a commonly used three-drug method causes excruciating pain, violating the Constitution's ban on cruel and unusual punishment.

Officials in Texas, Virginia and Alabama—three of the most active death penalty states—said they will soon restart the process.

Florida Attorney General Bill McCollum said he hopes Wednesday's ruling will allow the state to move forward with the execution of child killer Mark Dean Schwab.

In Virginia, where Governor Tim Kaine said executions will begin again, store clerk killer Kevin Green is scheduled to be executed on May 27.

The justices never officially imposed a moratorium. But within days of the Court's September 25 announcement that it would review lethal injections, lower-court judges began postponing executions to wait for a ruling. The justices themselves eventually blocked some executions, although they had allowed one to go through on the evening of September 25.

[U.S. Supreme Court] Chief Justice John Roberts, writing the main opinion, said the Kentucky inmates had failed to show that the three-drug method poses an unconstitutional risk of pain. He said prisoners who challenge a method as unconstitutional would have to show that it presented a "substantial risk" of harm to the prisoner. "Simply because an execution method may result in pain," Roberts wrote, "does not establish the sort of objectively intolerable risk of harm that qualifies as cruel and unusual."

[U.S. Supreme Court] Justices Anthony Kennedy and Samuel Alito joined his opinion. Justices John Paul Stevens and Stephen Breyer agreed that the inmates had not made the case that the system was flawed but disagreed with Roberts' rationale. Justices Clarence Thomas and Antonin Scalia also voted against the prisoners but said a method of execution would violate the Eighth Amendment only if it were "deliberately designed to inflict pain."

Justices Ruth Bader Ginsburg and David Souter dissented.

—Joan Biskupic; Kevin Johnson

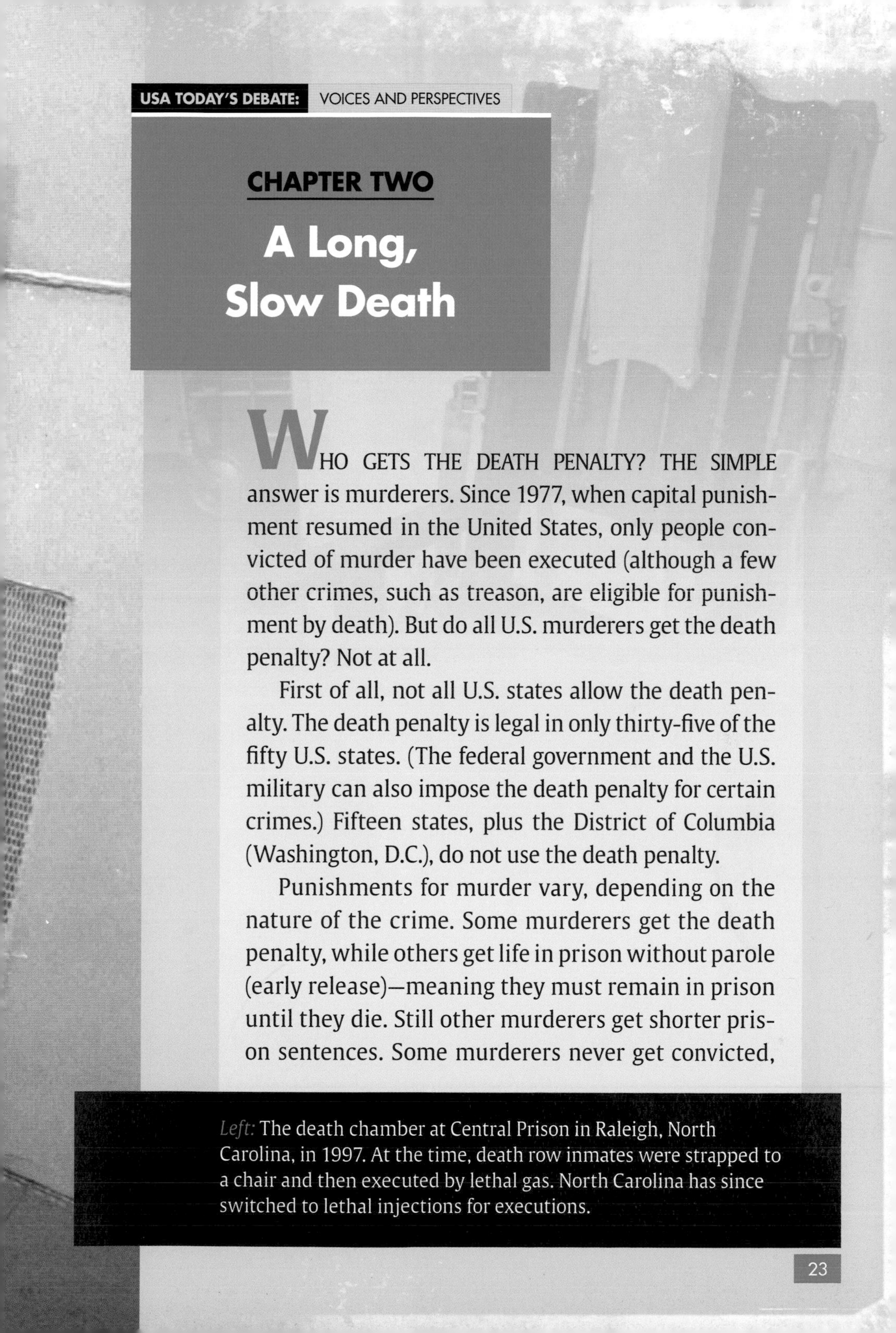

## CHAPTER TWO

# A Long, Slow Death

WHO GETS THE DEATH PENALTY? THE SIMPLE answer is murderers. Since 1977, when capital punishment resumed in the United States, only people convicted of murder have been executed (although a few other crimes, such as treason, are eligible for punishment by death). But do all U.S. murderers get the death penalty? Not at all.

First of all, not all U.S. states allow the death penalty. The death penalty is legal in only thirty-five of the fifty U.S. states. (The federal government and the U.S. military can also impose the death penalty for certain crimes.) Fifteen states, plus the District of Columbia (Washington, D.C.), do not use the death penalty.

Punishments for murder vary, depending on the nature of the crime. Some murderers get the death penalty, while others get life in prison without parole (early release)—meaning they must remain in prison until they die. Still other murderers get shorter prison sentences. Some murderers never get convicted,

*Left:* The death chamber at Central Prison in Raleigh, North Carolina, in 1997. At the time, death row inmates were strapped to a chair and then executed by lethal gas. North Carolina has since switched to lethal injections for executions.

or found guilty. Other murderers never get caught in the first place.

Consider the numbers. An estimated 16,000 murders take place each year in the United States. These murders result in about 13,000 arrests and 8,000 convictions. But of these 8,000 convictions, fewer than 120 murderers get death sentences, and not all death sentences are carried out. Between 1967 and 1997, the United States carried out just 1 execution for every 1,600 murders.

## DEATH ROW

States house inmates who have been sentenced to death in special facilities within high-security prisons. These facilities are commonly called death rows. Facilities vary from state to state. In most cases, death row is located far away from the rest of the prison, behind a series of locked doors and gates.

In North Carolina, male death row inmates live at Central Prison in Raleigh. Life there is highly regulated.

*Above:* Travis Walters is a death row inmate at Central Prison in Raleigh, North Carolina. Guards watch death row prisoners closely and give them only limited freedom of movement.

# The Federal Death Penalty

In addition to states, the federal government can impose the death penalty for federal crimes. Federal crimes that qualify for a death sentence include:

- Murder of a federal judge or law enforcement official
- Murder of a member of Congress
- Murder of a foreign official
- Espionage (spying for a foreign government)
- Treason
- Drug trafficking
- Terrorist murder of a U.S. citizen in a foreign country
- Murder by use of a weapon of mass destruction (a biological, chemical, or nuclear weapon)

Like the states, the federal government did not impose the death penalty between 1967 and 1977, while the Supreme Court considered whether the punishment violated the U.S. Constitution. The federal government reinstated the death penalty in 1988. It has carried out three executions since then. The first and most famous of those executed was Timothy McVeigh, the Oklahoma City bomber, responsible for the death of 168 people. Eight of those killed in the bombing were federal employees, which made McVeigh eligible for the federal death penalty. McVeigh died by lethal injection in 2001. The president of the United States has the authority to grant clemency in federal death penalty cases, just as governors do in state death penalty cases.

Inmates spend all day in small, single-person cells or in a common room. Each cell has a bed, a sink, a toilet, and a writing table. The common room holds tables and a television. Prison guards watch the inmates at all times, even when they shower or use the bathroom, to make sure they don't harm themselves, harm other inmates, or break prison rules. One hour a day is set aside for exercise. Inmates can receive two visitors per week, but they must speak to them only through bulletproof glass—no hugging or touching is allowed. Some inmates are assigned to prison jobs, such as laundry or janitorial work. Death row inmates who break prison rules are placed in segregation. They must eat meals in their cells and have no contact with other prisoners.

Many death row inmates have been abandoned by family and friends. Their connection to the outside world is through their attorneys and prison guards. Hovering over them at all times are feelings of fear, powerlessness, and the prospect of death. Joseph Giarratano, who lived on death row in Virginia from 1979 to 1991 (when his sentence was reduced), described his daily struggle this way:

> Hope is such a frail thing when hopelessness constantly bombards the senses. You can hear its empty sound in the clanging of the steel doors, in the rattle of chains, in the body searches, in the lack of privacy, in the night sounds of death row, and you can see it in the eyes of the guards who never really look at you, but are always watching [you]. You can feel the hopelessness each time you are asked to state your number, when you are holding the hand of a friend in chains who is being pulled away from you, never to be seen again. You can hear it in the echo of a system where humanity is constantly denied.... [H]ere on the row, where life goes on, death is never distant. Here life and death are one.

Death row is not all hopelessness and despair. Many prisoners use their time productively. Some take part in prison programs that allow them to earn a high school or college degree. Others study law books, hoping to gain knowledge that will help them fight their death sentences. Still others devote their lives to religion. For instance, Karla Tucker arrived on death row in Texas as a drug-addicted murderer, convicted of butchering two people with a pickax. During her fifteen years on death row, Tucker became a born-again Christian and a model prisoner. James Allridge taught other inmates to read and write and taught himself to paint and draw. He even sold some of his artwork, using the profits to help pay his legal fees. During his years on death row, Tookie Williams wrote children's books, encouraging young people to stay away from drugs and gangs.

## THE APPEALS SYSTEM

Like all people convicted of crimes, prisoners on death row have the right to appeal their sentences. That is, they have the right to ask a higher court to review their cases. People sentenced to death almost always appeal their sentences. Many states also automatically appeal death sentences to a higher court. The appeals process is designed to prevent unfair sentences or punishment of an innocent person.

When reviewing a case on appeal, the higher court considers

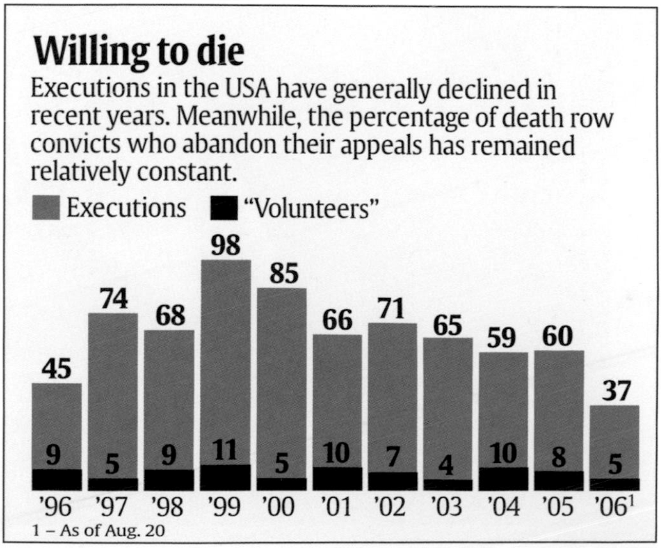


Source: Death Penalty Information Center By Alejandro Gonzalez, USA TODAY, 2006

whether the lower court's sentence was fair. The higher court might review whether police or lawyers acted within the law in handling the case. It might also look at new evidence that casts doubt on the guilt of the accused person. Every state has at least one appeals court, plus a state supreme court. Sometimes death row inmates appeal their cases to the federal level, all the way to the U.S. Supreme Court, the highest court in the nation.

Thomas Capano's case is typical of many death penalty cases. In 1999 the Delaware Superior Court sentenced Capano to death for the murder of Anne Marie Fahey. Capano appealed his sentence to the Delaware Supreme Court. In 2006 the higher court ruled that Capano's death sentence had violated a 2002 U.S. Supreme Court ruling dealing with juries in death penalty cases. Because of this violation, the court changed Capano's sentence to life in prison without parole.

*Above:* Thomas Capano *(right)* leaves the courthouse during the penalty phase of his murder trial, which resulted in a death sentence. The Delaware Supreme Court later changed the sentence to life without parole.

# Trial by Jury

After a capital crime, it is up to prosecutors (attorneys in charge of convicting criminals) to decide whether or not to pursue the death penalty in the case. If a prosecutor does choose to seek the death penalty, in most states the trial takes place before a twelve-person jury.

Death penalty cases are divided into two parts: the conviction phase, in which the jury decides whether the defendant is innocent or guilty, and the sentencing phase, in which the jury decides whether the defendant should be executed. In most states, the jury's vote must be unanimous—meaning all jurors must agree. (In some states, a judge can override the jury's decision on sentencing.)

Juries are made up of ordinary citizens, chosen at random from lists of voters or taxpayers. The jury selection process begins with a "jury pool" of fifty people or more. Using interviews and questionnaires, court staff, judges, and attorneys gradually whittle this group down to twelve jurors and one or two alternates to fill in if a regular juror gets sick.

In theory, the goal of jury selection is to find jurors who will be impartial in making decisions. In reality, each side wants to win its case. So prosecutors look for jurors who are likely to convict, and defense attorneys look for jurors who will be sympathetic to their client. Prosecutors often try to fill juries with white men, who are more likely to convict than are women and minorities. Defense attorneys do just the opposite. In addition, the law requires that all jurors in death penalty cases be "death qualified," or willing to impose a death sentence. Therefore, jurors who are morally opposed to the death penalty are automatically disqualified from serving on death penalty cases.

## WAITING GAME

In death row cases, prisoners and their attorneys commonly file appeal after appeal, hoping to reverse death sentences. The system is slow, and the process often drags on for ten years or more. The lengthy appeals system ensures that prisoners have adequate chances to prove their innocence in the case of a wrongful conviction. But the long-drawn-out process can be agonizing for everyone involved in a death penalty case.

Victims' families suffer on many levels. First, they must endure the heartbreaking murder of a loved one. They often feel grief, rage, despair, and a desire for revenge. Many want to see their loved one's murderer put to death, and they follow the appeals process closely. As the process moves forward, families must negotiate a maze of technical language and complex legal procedures. They often feel ignored, confused, and frustrated. Some victims' relatives must give court testimony about the murder, a process that opens painful wounds.

Consider the family of state trooper Mark Frederick. In 1976 Billy George Hughes shot Frederick on a Texas highway. In 1997, after fifty-five court appearances, Hughes was still on death row, and Frederick's family was still waiting for justice. "I just thought the system worked;

*Above:* Victims' families listen to a killer make a final statement during sentencing. The long trial and appeals process can be heartbreaking for victims' families.

that there would be a trial, and then there would be a couple of appeals at the state and the federal [levels]. . . . I had no idea that twenty-one years later, that I would be going through the process," said Frederick's mother, Pat Teer. Hughes was executed in 2000, twenty-four years after committing his crime.

For inmates, the appeals system is also difficult. It traps them in a nearly endless sea of paperwork, of soaring ups and devastating downs. Ellis Wayne Felker was sentenced to die for a 1981 murder. He lived on Georgia's death row for thirteen years while attorneys tried to prove his innocence. He received four stays of execution—that is, four times he was scheduled for death and four times the execution was called off. Each time, Felker was probably relieved to be saved and disheartened when his execution was rescheduled. He finally died by electrocution on November 15, 1996, one day after his fourth and final stay of execution.

> **"The lapse of time of over two decades between sentence and the imposition of sentence is unacceptable. To require the family of the victims to wait over 20 years . . . only adds to their pain and suffering."**
>
> —**WILLIAM BRATTON,** LOS ANGELES POLICE CHIEF
>
> USA TODAY · JULY 1, 2008

In general, Americans dislike the lengthy appeals system. They think the system is inefficient, a waste of money, and a delay of justice. After all, a few inmates live on death row for more than twenty years.

USA TODAY
News
SECTION A

July 24, 2008

# Prisoners' Death Row Time Doubles

From the Pages of USA TODAY

THE TIME PRISONERS SPEND on death row has nearly doubled during the past two decades. Legal experts predict it will rise further as states review execution procedures and prisoners pursue lengthy appeals.

Waits rose from seven years in 1986 to twelve years in 2006, the latest [U.S.] Justice Department statistics show. In all five states with the most prisoners on death row—California, Florida, Texas, Pennsylvania and Alabama—offenders spend more time in prison than they did four years ago, a USA TODAY survey of state records through 2007 found.

In California, wait times average nearly 20 years, a state commission report in June says. It costs about $90,000 more per year to house a death row inmate than other inmates.

In April [2008], the U.S. Supreme Court upheld Kentucky's lethal injection method, ending an informal halt to executions nationwide for seven months. Of the 10 states with the most prisoners on death row, five launched their own reviews of lethal injection procedures in the past two years. Those resulted in suspensions or delays in executions.

Fordham University law professor Deborah Denno says lethal injection challenges create a "snowball effect" that prolongs death row waits.

Lengthy appeals by prisoners slow executions. "Death penalty cases should be the highest priority for the courts," says Clay Crenshaw, chief of Alabama's death penalty litigation unit. "It isn't any more." Crenshaw says courts take about five years to rule on appeals. The three offenders executed in Alabama in 2007 spent an average of 23 years on death row.

The wait times amount to prisoners getting "two distinct punishments": the death sentence and years in solitary confinement, says Richard Dieter of the Death Penalty Information Center, which opposes the death penalty.

The California commission said excessive delays had rendered the nation's largest death penalty system "dysfunctional" and in danger of collapse.

"Death row was only supposed to be temporary," Denno says. "Now we have inmates on death row for more than a quarter-century."

—Kevin Johnson

Despite efforts to streamline the process, prisoners are spending more and more time on death row. In 1990 the average time between sentencing and execution was seven years. By 2008 the time had increased to 12.7 years.

## LAST CHANCE

After all appeals have been exhausted, prisoners on death row still have one last chance to avoid execution. They can request clemency—a lessening of punishment—from the state governor. The governor may grant clemency for any reason, but the most common reasons are lingering doubt about the guilt of the accused, the governor's personal opposition to the death penalty, or the mental impairment of the accused. Clemency laws differ from state to state. Some governors have sole power to grant or deny clemency. Other governors must act with advice from boards of pardons and paroles.

Since 1977 about one thousand death-row inmates have sought clemency from state governors. Governors have granted clemency to about 250 inmates. However, 167 of those clemencies came all at once—when Illinois governor George Ryan emptied his state's death row in 2003. Death row inmates who receive clemency do not go free. They remain in prison for life but no longer face execution.

Several recent clemency requests have made headlines. Those of Karla Faye Tucker and

> **"I still believe the death penalty is a proper response to heinous crimes. But I want to make sure . . . that the person who is put to death is absolutely guilty."**
>
> **—GEORGE RYAN,** ILLINOIS GOVERNOR, AFTER DECLARING A MORATORIUM ON EXECUTIONS IN HIS STATE, 2000

Tookie Williams were unsuccessful. Robin Lovitt, who was scheduled to become the one thousandth person executed since 1977, was successful in his request for clemency. Lovitt's lawyers argued to Virginia governor Mark Warner that evidence that might have proven Lovitt's innocence had been improperly destroyed. In 2005 Warner agreed that Lovitt deserved clemency and commuted his sentence to life in prison without parole.

*Above:* Karla Faye Tucker was executed in 1997 for her role in a double murder. Her requests for clemency were denied.

## THE LAST DAYS

If all appeals and requests for clemency are unsuccessful, the death row prisoner will be executed. In North Carolina's Central Prison, inmates leave their cells three to seven days before their scheduled executions. They move to the prison's "death watch" area, located near the execution chamber. On death watch, prisoners spend all day in a cell, except for fifteen minutes allowed for showering. Two guards watch them twenty-four hours a day. They have no contact with other inmates, although visitors—including family members, lawyers, and religious counselors—are allowed.

Prisoners on Texas's death row move to death watch thirty-six hours before execution. There, prison staffers ask them a series of questions: What do you want for your last meal? Who will your last visitors be? Who will claim your property or any money in your prison bank account after death? Do you want to donate your body to the prison medical facility or will family members claim your body? Twenty-four hours before the execution, the prisoner is shackled and taken by van to a building called the Walls in downtown Huntsville, Texas. There, the prisoner can visit one last time with family, lawyers, and spiritual advisers. He or she eats a last meal at 4:30 P.M.

Texas carries out all executions by lethal injection. The procedure begins around 6:00 P.M. If there are no last-minute stays, prison staffers walk the inmate to the execution chamber. He or she lies on a gurney, a padded table with leather straps to secure the prisoner's head, arms, legs, and trunk. A medical team inserts IV needles into each of the prisoner's arms. Those who will witness the execution enter a small room with

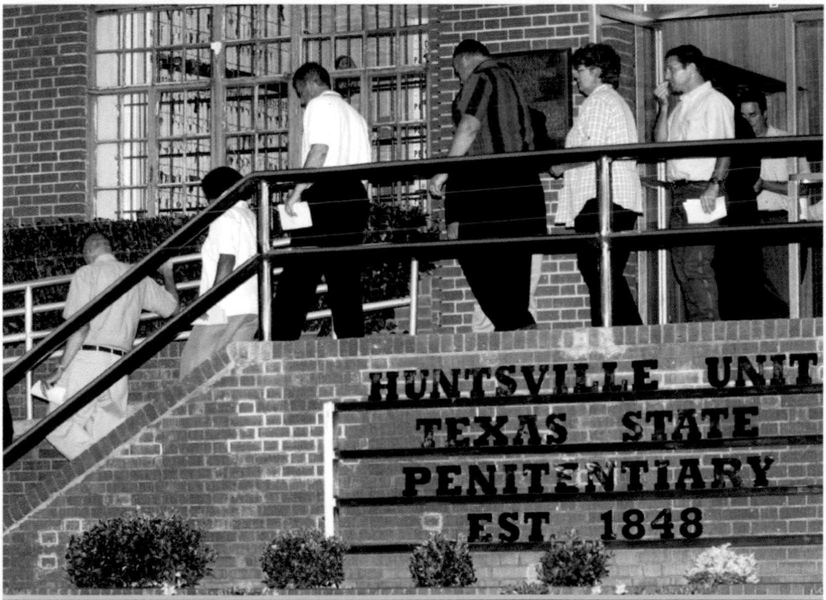


*Above:* The family of a murder victim exits a prison after the execution of the murderer in 2006.

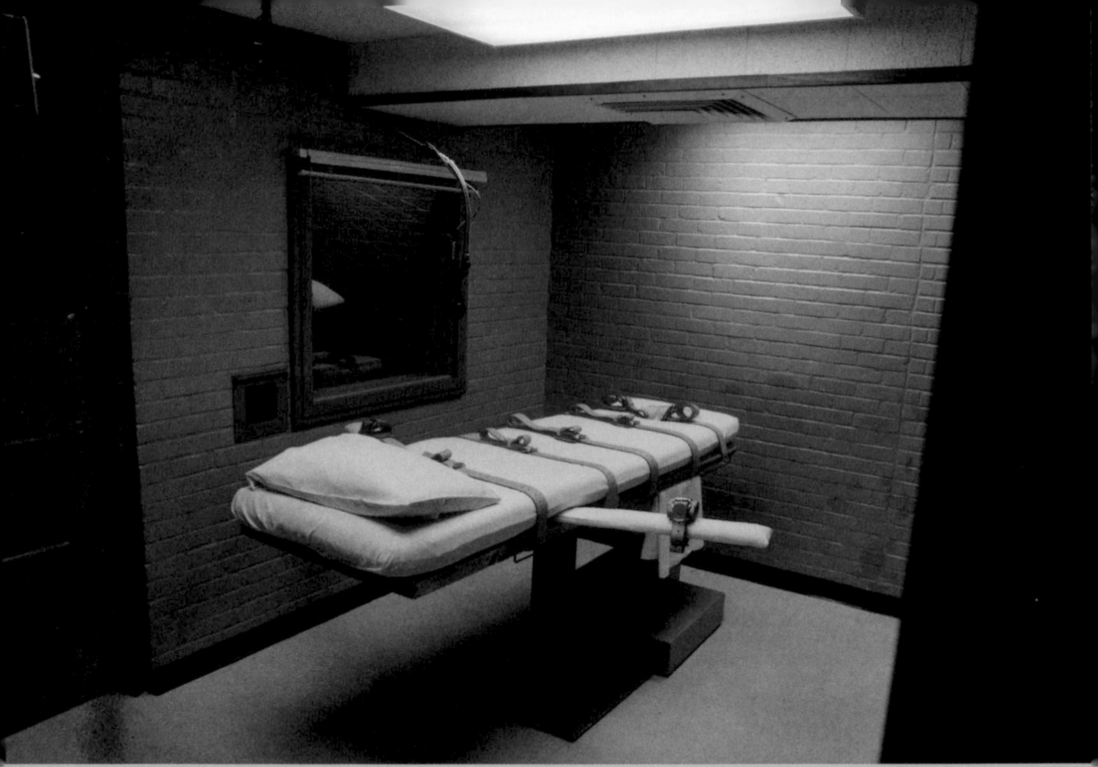

*Above:* Families and other witnesses can watch executions through windows looking into the death chamber.

a window onto the death chamber. Witnesses often include the prisoner's family members, victims' family members, clergypeople, and members of the media. The prison warden asks if the condemned person has any last words, which he or she speaks into a microphone hanging from the ceiling. Some prisoners apologize to their victims' families. Others declare their innocence. Some simply pray or say good-bye. Then the warden gives a signal to executioners behind a mirrored glass window. They begin the flow of lethal drugs that will kill the prisoner within minutes.

For witnesses and members of the execution team, the procedure can be disturbing. "I've had several of them [executed prisoners] where watching their last breath go from their bodies and their eyes never unfix from mine. I mean actually lock together," comments Jim Brazzil, a chaplain with the Texas Department of Criminal Justice. He continues, "I can close my eyes now and see those eyes. My feelings and emotions are extremely intense at that time. . . . I've never really been able to describe it." Victims' families who have hoped for years to see a death penalty carried out often sob in relief during the procedure. Prisoners' families may become extremely emotional, weeping and crying out as they watch a family member executed.

AT
12:01
SAN QUENTIN
CALIFORNIA
94964

USA TODAY'S DEBATE: VOICES AND PERSPECTIVES

## CHAPTER THREE

# Right and Wrong

THE DEBATE OVER CAPITAL PUNISHMENT IS highly personal and emotional. It involves differing views about right and wrong, justice and injustice. Those who support capital punishment and those who oppose capital punishment agree on one thing: killing is wrong. But there the agreement ends.

### "AN EYE FOR AN EYE"

The desire for vengeance is human. The biblical saying "an eye for an eye, a tooth for a tooth" reflects this desire. In fact, many people cite this and other biblical passages when expressing support for the death penalty. Those who support capital punishment make a simple and

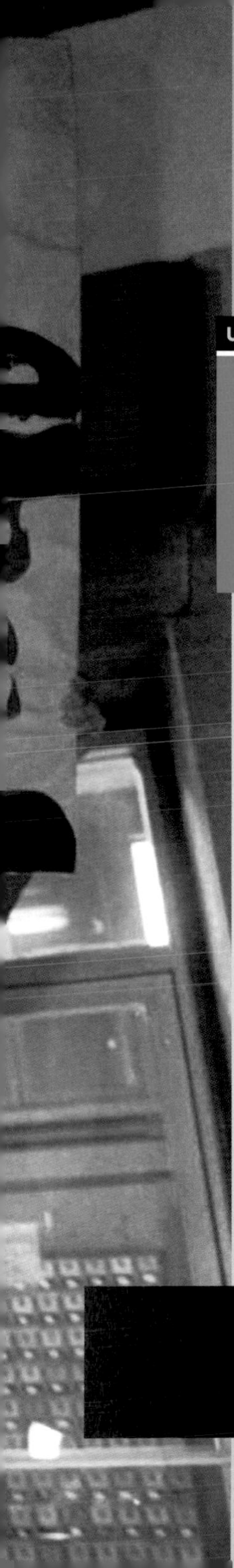

*Left:* A death penalty supporter makes his view known outside of San Quentin State Prison in California after an execution in the late 1990s.

straightforward argument. Taking a life is so despicable, they believe, that a murderer should pay the ultimate price—death—for his or her crime. "Those who commit such atrocities . . . forfeit their own right to live," writes Alex Kozinski, a judge on the U.S. Court of Appeals for the Ninth Circuit in California. "We tarnish the memory of the dead and heap needless misery on their surviving families by letting the perpetrators live."

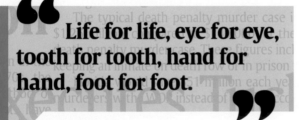

> **"Life for life, eye for eye, tooth for tooth, hand for hand, foot for foot."**
>
> **—HEBREW BIBLE,** EXODUS 21:24

Related to this argument is the concept of vengeance, or payback. Those who support capital punishment believe that killers should suffer because they have made others suffer. Judge Kozinski explains, "I believe that society is entitled to take the life of those who have shown utter contempt for the lives of others. And because I hear the tortured voices of the victims crying out to me for vindication [vengeance]."

Families of victims are most likely to express the desire for vengeance. Russell Nelson, a twenty-one-year-old college student, was one of thirty-three victims tortured and killed by serial killer John Wayne Gacy. "It's so damn hard," said Russell's mother, Norma, in 1990. "[Russell's murder is] the first thing you think of in the morning and the last thing you think of at night. . . . I think they should [do to Gacy] the same thing he did to [his victims]—torture him to death."

Some family members are even tempted to take the law into their own hands. When Clarence Hill, convicted of killing Florida police officer Stephen Taylor, received a last-minute stay of execution in 2006, Taylor's family was weary and frustrated. They had been waiting twenty-four years for Hill's execution. "If they want me to, I'd put a bullet in his brain," said Jack Taylor, brother of the slain officer.

Anger such as this is a common reaction to the murder of a loved one. That's why most states that use the death penalty allow victim's family members to witness executions. The theory is that seeing a killer executed can provide some satisfaction or relief for families.

Brooks Douglass was sixteen years old when two men entered his family farmhouse in Oklahoma in 1979. They tied up Douglass and his parents, then raped Douglass's twelve-year-old sister in another room. Next, the two men sat down and ate the family's dinner before shooting all four family members in the back. Douglass and his sister survived, but their parents died.

The killers were sentenced to death. As they filed appeal after appeal, Douglass seethed with grief and anger. He got involved in the movement for victims' rights. This movement attempts to give victims' families more involvement in the death penalty cases, for instance, by telling death penalty jurors about their pain and suffering during sentencing and by viewing executions. In 1990 Douglass won a seat in the Oklahoma State Senate, where he sponsored many victims' rights bills.

In 1996 Douglass and his sister witnessed the execution of one of the two killers, Steven Hatch. After the execution, Douglass remarked that Hatch, killed by lethal injection, had died too easily. "I was criticized for fostering revenge," Douglass says. "So what? Who are we to question what a person's feelings are when they go view an execution? There is no other party that has more to benefit from seeing the killer executed than a family member."

## A FITTING PUNISHMENT?

In states that don't have capital punishment, the most severe legal punishment is life in prison without parole (LWOP). Is this a fitting punishment for a brutal crime? Death penalty supporters say no. Prisons are paid for by taxpayer dollars. Some argue:

Why should taxpayers foot the bill for housing, feeding, clothing, and caring for the health needs of convicted murderers, often for decades on end?

"I'm very disappointed in the American justice system," said Marion Lewis after a jury sentenced Lee Boyd Malvo to life in prison instead of the death penalty for his part in the Washington, D.C., shootings. Lewis's daughter, Lori Ann Lewis-Rivera, had been one of Malvo's ten murdered victims. Lewis continued, "Our society has now been sentenced to the responsibility of seeing to this man's health and welfare for the next 30 or 40 years, and that's unconscionable [unjust]." Although life in prison is a harsh punishment, victims' families especially note that their loved ones have no life at all.

Take the case of Dennis Rader. Known as the BTK killer (because he bound, tortured, and killed his victims), Rader viciously murdered ten people in the Wichita, Kansas, area between 1974 and 1991. One of his victims was only nine years old.

The court found Rader guilty but could not sentence him to death for his crimes, because by law, Kansas could not impose the death penalty for any murders committed before 1994. Instead of death, Rader received ten life sentences—one for each of his victims—with no possibility of parole.

"I hungered for a death penalty in that case," said Nola Foulston, the lead attorney in charge of convicting Rader. Beverly Plapp, the sister of one of Rader's victims, was more emotional. "As far as I'm concerned, Dennis Rader does not deserve to live," she told reporters. "I want him to suffer as much as he made his victims suffer. This man needs to be thrown in a deep, dark hole and left to rot."

## WHO SPEAKS FOR THE VICTIMS?

In Kentucky in 2000, a group of nuns wanted to protest capital punishment. They encouraged churches to ring their bells for two minutes on the day of an execution anywhere in the United States. Some death penalty supporters scoffed at this idea. Why ring bells for murderers? they asked. Why not ring bells instead for innocent murder victims? After all, thousands more die each year at the hands of murderers than at the hands of state executioners.

Death penalty supporters have little sympathy for someone who takes an innocent life. They think the media and the criminal justice system focus too much on death row inmates—on whether they are treated fairly, on whether their appeals are handled properly. "Everything is Billy Hughes' rights. He has one right—another right—another right—another right," commented Pat Teer, who waited through twenty-four years and fifty-five court appearances before Hughes, her son's killer, was put to death. She added that when Hughes shot her son, state trooper Mark Frederick, "Mark didn't have any rights."

From the perspective of death penalty supporters, killers seem to get all the attention, while their victims get almost none. Take the case of Mumia Abu-Jamal, a black man convicted of killing Philadelphia police officer Daniel Faulkner in 1981. According to evidence and eyewitnesses, when Faulkner tried to arrest Abu-Jamal's brother, Abu-Jamal shot Faulkner in the back and then repeatedly shot him in the face.

*Above:* Protesters march on behalf of Mumia Abu-Jamal in Los Angeles, California, in 2000.

# Victims' Rights

Laws regarding crime victims' rights vary from state to state. In most states, these laws address issues such as victims' privacy, police treatment of victims, victims' involvement in criminal trials, and medical treatment for crime victims. Here are some of the rights guaranteed to crime victims in Oklahoma or the families of victims in death penalty cases:

The right . . .

- To be notified that a court proceeding to which the victim has been summoned will or will not go on as scheduled, in order to prevent an unnecessary trip to court
- To receive protection from harm and threats of harm arising out of cooperation with law enforcement and prosecution efforts, and to be provided with information about how to access protection
- To be informed of financial assistance and other social services available to victims
- To be provided, whenever possible, with a secure waiting area during court proceedings, at a distance from defendants and families and friends of defendants
- To be informed of any plea bargain negotiations (in which the defendant pleads guilty in exchange for a reduced charge)
- To have victim impact statements filed with the court
- To be informed if a sentence is overturned or modified
- To be notified of Pardon and Parole Board actions

Abu-Jamal was sentenced to death. But during his years on death row, he has become an international celebrity. People display his picture on T-shirts, posters, and tote bags. Citizens in Saint-Denis, a suburb of faraway Paris, France, have named a street in his honor. Rock groups have thrown benefit concerts for him. He's written books and newspaper articles in prison. World leaders, famous writers, and Hollywood actors have all championed his cause. They say he's an innocent man who was wrongly convicted by a racially biased criminal justice system.

*Above:* Daniel Faulkner's murder is often overlooked in the publicity surrounding his murderer, Mumia Abu-Jamal.

But many people ask, What about Daniel Faulkner, the officer Abu-Jamal murdered? Who remembers him? His picture is not on T-shirts or tote bags. No celebrities or rock stars pay him honors.

In 1994 National Public Radio announced that it had signed Abu-Jamal to do radio commentaries about life in prison. For Faulkner's widow, Maureen, that was the last straw. She said the station shouldn't give a voice to a convicted cop killer. The radio station answered that Abu-Jamal had a constitutional right to freedom of speech. "Well, what about my husband, who is six feet under?" Maureen Faulkner answered. "He's lost his ability for his freedom of speech."

April 15, 1996

# Why I Want to Watch a Killer Die

From the Pages of USA TODAY

It is not retaliation or retribution that I seek in witnessing the execution of the man who killed my parents. It is closure. Closure on an era of my life into which I never chose to enter. Closure of years of anger and hate.

In the past 20 years, the criminal justice system has made great advances in protecting the rights of defendants [people on trial for a crime]. The rights and procedures that resulted are critical to any system of justice which is based on the presumption of innocence.

However, as we protect the defendant's rights, we often allow the system to literally step over the body of the victim to read the defendant his rights. Ideally, the purpose of the criminal justice system should be to punish the offenders while allowing the victim to go on with his life.

I discovered this the hard way.

One October evening in 1979, my parents were killed by two men who broke into our home in Okarche, a small town west of Oklahoma City. They came to rob, and raped my sister who was then 12 years old. I was shot in the back. My sister also was shot. I was 16.

Over the next seven years, I testified seven times at trials and retrials. Each time, my life was completely disrupted as I relived that evening over and over again.

In all those times, I was never once allowed to tell the jury anything but the facts. The jury never heard of the struggles I faced in life because I didn't have parents. I was never able to tell what it feels like to spend holidays alone.

Despite these events, I still had a life to live. I graduated from law school, started my own business and was elected to the Oklahoma Senate at age 27. As a senator, I wanted to work for a criminal justice system that's fair to defendants and victims and that allows victims the chance to move on with their lives.

In order to have such a system, the victim must be a part of and believe in the system. If these two things occur, the victim can find closure and begin to move on.

First, the victim must have the opportunity to participate in the system.

Simply notifying a victim of hearings is a step that results in the victim feeling a part of the process. In any lawsuit, parties are required to notify the other party of developments. Yet in many states, victims are not notified of events as crucial as parole hearings.

Another step that allows a victim to participate is the victim's impact statement. In the sentencing phase, victims or their families testify about the crime's emotional, psychological and physical effects. Testifying gives the victim a chance to be heard. Voicing these feelings allows the victim to feel a part of and in turn accept the outcome of the process.

Accepting the outcome brings about the second step of healing. A victim must believe in the system. He must believe that criminals will be accountable for their actions. And he needs the assurance that the sentence will be carried out.

If the victim must constantly look over his shoulder or is continually brought back to court to testify, he has no realistic way of overcoming the hurt.

Once the victim believes justice is served, the victim can find closure. Closure is something each person must find for himself. I can't prescribe treatment, nor can I legislate it.

Recently, I was able to talk to one of the men who broke into our home. Meeting with [Glen] Ake [one of the murderers, whose death sentence was changed to life in prison] was one of the most emotional and dramatic experiences of my life. I was finally able to release the anger and hate. I was finally able to have a day when my thoughts didn't involve these men.

Ake was very remorseful. I choked up when I saw him, and the first thing he said was: "I want you to know that I am so, so sorry about what I did to you and your family."

I watched his every movement, and I feel he was sincere. Forgiveness gave me closure with Ake. To me forgiveness doesn't mean that Ake should be released, nor does it mean Hatch [the other killer] shouldn't die. Both are accountable to society for their actions. I found closure with Ake when I met him face to face.

I believe I will find closure with Hatch watching him die.

—Brooks Douglass, Oklahoma state senator

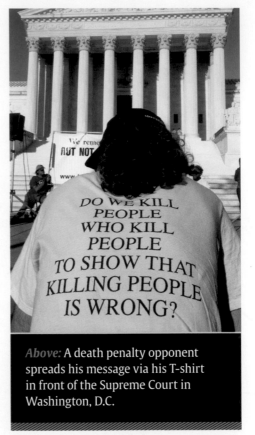

*Above:* A death penalty opponent spreads his message via his T-shirt in front of the Supreme Court in Washington, D.C.

### "LOVE YOUR ENEMIES"

Like death penalty supporters, death penalty opponents hold strong beliefs about right and wrong. Those who oppose the death penalty say it is wrong for anyone—including the government—to take a human life. They argue that capital punishment only makes a society more brutal, savage, and uncivilized. "There is a better response to killing than killing," argues Mario Cuomo, former governor of New York. A popular bumper sticker asks: "Why do we kill people who kill people to show people that killing people is wrong?"

The Hebrew Bible, or Old Testament, talks about "eye for eye, tooth for tooth." But the Christian Bible, or New Testament, talks about forgiveness. Many who oppose the death penalty point to the New Testament to guide their beliefs. For example, in the biblical book of Matthew, part of the New Testament, the religious teacher Jesus says:

> You have heard that it was said, "Eye for eye, and tooth for tooth." But I tell you, Do not resist an evil person. If someone strikes you on the right cheek, turn to him the other also. . . . You have heard that it was said, "Love your neighbor and hate your enemy." But I tell you: Love your enemies."

# Crusader: Sister Helen Prejean

Sister Helen Prejean, a Catholic nun, is a leading voice in the anti–death penalty movement. In 1982, as part of her work with the poor, she met Patrick Sonnier, a convicted murderer living on death row at the Louisiana State Penitentiary. Prejean became Sonnier's spiritual adviser in the months leading up to his execution. Through her experiences with Sonnier, Prejean grew more and more alarmed about the flaws and injustices of the U.S. death penalty system. She became a crusader to end capital punishment. Prejean has written two books. The first, *Dead Man Walking* (1993), tells of her friendship with Patrick Sonnier. The book was made into a 1996 motion picture starring Susan Sarandon as Sister Helen and Sean Penn as a character based on Sonnier. Prejean's second book, *The Death of Innocents: An Eyewitness Account of Wrongful Executions* (2004), follows the stories of two men whom Prejean believes were innocent of the crimes for which they were executed.

*Above:* Sister Helen Prejean has been crusading against the death penalty for more than twenty-five years.

The Catholic Church takes a strong stand against the death penalty. In a 1980 "Statement on Capital Punishment," U.S. Catholic bishops wrote that abolishing the death penalty "sends a message that we can break the cycle of violence, that we need not take life for life, that we can envisage [imagine] more humane and more hopeful and effective responses to the growth of violent crime." The bishops also stressed the preciousness and sanctity of all human life and said that it was up to individuals to safeguard life, not to destroy it.

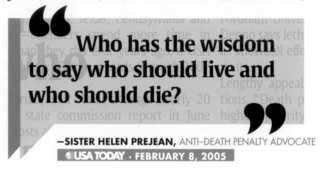

> **"Who has the wisdom to say who should live and who should die?"**
>
> —SISTER HELEN PREJEAN, ANTI–DEATH PENALTY ADVOCATE
> USA TODAY · FEBRUARY 8, 2005

This message of forgiveness is not limited to religious Christians. It is a universal message that appeals to people of many faiths and backgrounds.

## THE CASE FOR COMPASSION

September 11, 2001, is a day that Americans will never forget. On that day, terrorists flew two passenger airplanes into the World Trade Center towers in New York City and another plane into the Pentagon near Washington, D.C. A fourth plane was headed for either the White House or the U.S. Capitol, but it crashed in a field in Pennsylvania after passengers fought back against the hijackers. All together, the September 11 attacks killed about three thousand people.

Mark Bingham died on the plane that crashed in Pennsylvania. His mother, Alice Hoagland, might have desired vengeance for al-Qaeda, the terrorist organization that carried out the September 11 attacks. But Hoagland took a different approach. She argued against the death penalty for Zacarias Moussaoui, an al-Qaeda member convicted in 2006 of helping plan the attacks. Hoagland stated:

> We Americans have the opportunity to demonstrate our compassion toward a man who has shown no compassion for America. We are a nation of laws, of justice, and of mercy. By sparing his life, we can demonstrate our humanity by acknowledging the humanity of a human being who badly needs compassion. By sparing his life, we will have overcome the sort of hatred that he displays toward us. . . . I hope that we as a nation can demonstrate our higher impulses by sparing his life—while keeping him safely behind bars for the remainder of his life. If we can do that, we will honor our own high standard of reverence for all life, and we will model a better standard of behavior for Zacarias Moussaoui to take to heart.

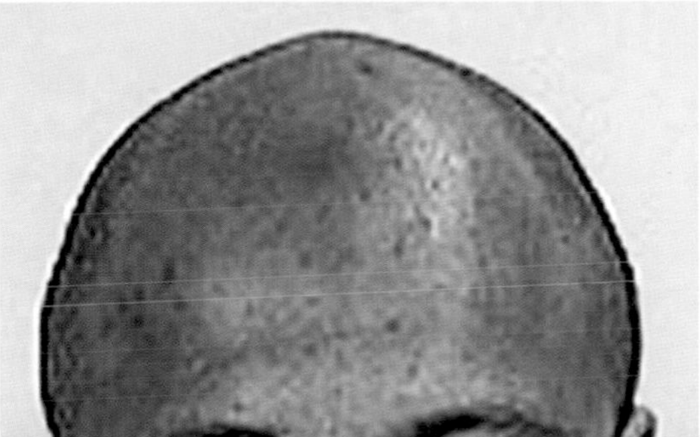

A jury decided that Zacarias Moussaoui *(above)*, a planner of the 9/11 terrorist attacks, should not get the death penalty for his crimes.

In the end, jurors in a federal trial decided on life in prison without parole instead of the death penalty for Moussaoui.

# A New Approach to Justice

In recent years, a movement called restorative justice has entered the arena of crime and punishment. Restorative justice steers away from the traditional pattern of punishment and revenge. Instead, it tries to reduce the atmosphere of violence that leads to crime in the first place. Restorative justice programs use a groundbreaking technique of bringing victims and offenders together for face-to-face dialogue. Victims are able to express their pain and suffering and move toward forgiveness, and offenders are able to better understand the impact of their crimes and move toward remorse and apology. In murder cases, offenders speak with victims' family members. Many anti–death penalty groups, including Murder Victims' Families for Human Rights, have embraced restorative justice ideals in their work.

*Above:* James Jones is bringing restorative justice to the Internet age with Oasis. This website links victims and offenders in a controlled environment and can lay the groundwork for face-to-face meetings.

**ABOUT FACE**

It's not uncommon for people to change their opinion about the death penalty, especially after firsthand experience with murder and execution. Overseeing executions was part of the job for Don Cabana, warden of the Mississippi State Penitentiary in the 1980s. But the realities of taking someone's life became unbearable for Cabana. He quit his job as warden after two executions and became a death penalty opponent.

Bud Welch also underwent a radical change of opinion. Welch's daughter, Julie, was killed in the Oklahoma City bombing in 1995. "For the first few months after Julie's death, all I could think about was getting McVeigh [the bomber]." Welch recalls. "It was good that when they brought him from the jail to the courthouse they put a lead vest on him, because I would have easily, gladly, taken a shot at him. I was consumed with anger."

But in the years following the bombing, Welch's feelings began to change. He remembered that Julie had once denounced the death penalty as "nothing but vengeance; it just fuels hate." Eventually, Welch decided that "killing McVeigh would only dishonor Julie." "I honor the sanctity of all life, not just innocent life, but mass murderers, too," he said. Welch went on to join Murder Victims' Families for Human Rights, an anti–death penalty group.

STOP

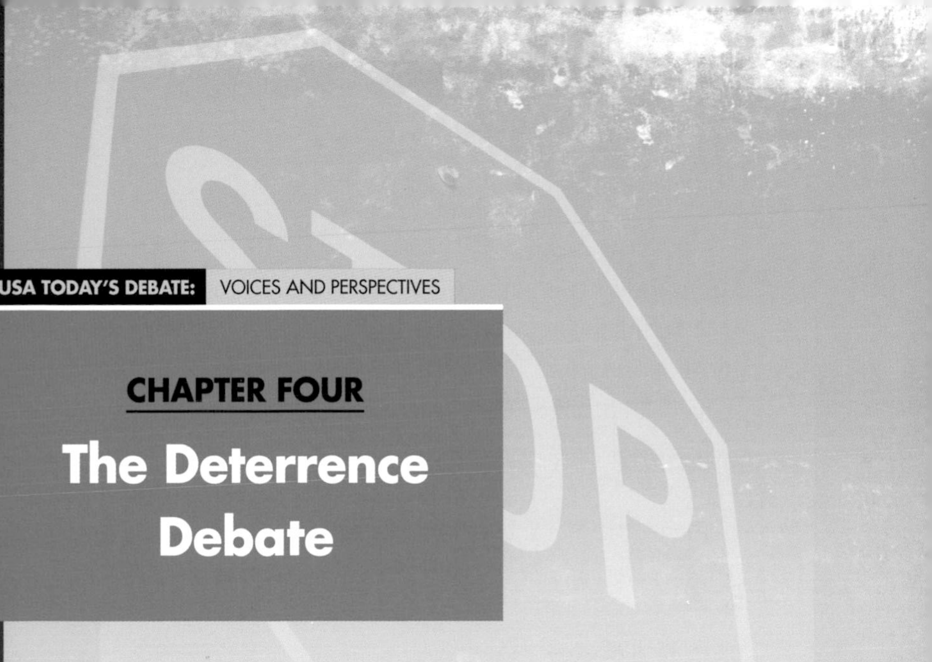


## CHAPTER FOUR

# The Deterrence Debate

MANY DEATH PENALTY SUPPORTERS CLAIM that capital punishment is a deterrent. The theory is that someone will choose not to commit murder, knowing that he or she might face the death penalty for the crime. In this way, the threat of capital punishment will deter murders, saving many innocent lives. Does this theory hold water? It depends on whom you ask.

### "YOU WILL BE PUNISHED"

Those who believe that capital punishment has a deterrent effect base their arguments on both statistics and common sense. Edward Koch, former mayor of New York City, discussed the issue in a 1985 essay in the *New Republic* magazine.

*Left:* Death penalty supporters believe that capital punishment stops would-be murderers from taking a life. Opponents believe capital punishment has no deterrent effects.

Koch said:

> Life is indeed precious, and I believe the death penalty helps to affirm this fact. Had the death penalty been a real possibility in the minds of these murderers, they might well have stayed their hand. They might have shown moral awareness before their victims died, and not after. Consider the tragic death of Rosa Velez, who happened to be home when a man named Luis Vera burglarized her apartment in Brooklyn. "Yeah, I shot her," Vera admitted. ". . . I knew I wouldn't go to the [electric] chair."

At the time of Koch's essay, the state of New York didn't have the death penalty. New York politician George Pataki thought that was a mistake. After Pataki become governor in 1995, New York reinstated the death penalty. By 1997 New York was seeing a decrease in violent crime. Pataki credited the death penalty and other tough laws with keeping crime down. He wrote:

*Above:* New York governor George Pataki helped reinstate the death penalty in New York in 1995. The state later abolished the death penalty.

> For too long, coddling of criminals allowed unacceptable levels of violence to permeate [fill] the streets. [Criminals] were not

> subject to swift and certain punishment and, as a result, violent criminal acts were not deterred. . . . No more. In New York, the death penalty has turned the tables on fear and put it back where it belongs—in the hearts of criminals. Within just one year, the death penalty helped produce a dramatic drop in violent crime . . . murders have dropped by nearly one-third. . . . I believe this has occurred in part because of the strong signal that the death penalty and our other tough new laws sent to violent criminals and murderers: You will be punished with the full force of the law.

In 1985 Stephen K. Layson, an economist at the University of North Carolina, published a study about the deterrent effects of capital punishment. His data showed that every execution of a murderer prevented about eighteen additional murders. In the early 2000s, economics professors at Clemson University in South Carolina and Emory University in Georgia carried out a similar study. This study also concluded that each execution resulted in eighteen fewer murders.

Perhaps the most dramatic statistics come from the years 1965 to 1980. During most of those years, executions were not allowed in the United States. And during the same period, murders doubled in the United States, shooting up from 9,960 to 23,040 per year. To death penalty supporters, the cause and effect are obvious: When criminals knew they would not be executed for their crimes, they committed many more murders.

What's more, as executions increased in the 1990s, U.S. murder rates dropped by 44 percent. In 1991 the murder rate in Texas was 15.3 murders for every 100,000 people. By 1999 the rate had fallen to 6.1 per 100,000—a drop of 60 percent. In Harris County, Texas, where officials aggressively pursued the death penalty, murder rates dropped by 72 percent from 1982 to 2002.

USA TODAY
News
SECTION A

January 7, 2003

# Death Penalty Gains Unlikely Defenders

From the Pages of USA TODAY

Robert Blecker sat quietly as other professors ticked off their reasons for opposing the death penalty: It's unfair to blacks. It doesn't really deter crime. Innocent people could be executed.

But Blecker, a professor at New York Law School, was having none of it. When it was his turn to speak at the recent death-penalty forum at John Jay College, he summed up his support for executions in three words: "Barbara Jo Brown."

Blecker then launched into a staccato description of the 11-year-old Louisiana girl's slaying in 1981, how she was abducted, raped and tortured by a man who later was executed. The story drew gasps from a crowd accustomed to dealing in legal theories and academic formulas. "We know evil when we see it, and it's past time that we start saying so," Blecker said later. "When it comes to the death penalty, too many in academia can't face that."

For years, professors and civil rights leaders have led the charge against the death penalty, raising questions about its fairness that caused two states to suspend executions. But now death-penalty supporters have found some unlikely allies: a small but growing number of professors and social scientists who are speaking out in favor of the ultimate sanction.

Challenging themes that have been the foundation of the anti-death penalty movement, about a dozen professors and social scientists have produced unprecedented research arguing that the penalty deters crime. The pro-death penalty researchers are still a tiny minority in U.S. academia, which Blecker guesses is "99%-plus" against executions. But the researchers are changing the nature of the death-penalty debate.

Justice Department lawyers have cited their work in legal briefs defending the death penalty. Republican senators have used the new research to try to stave off proposals to make it more difficult to execute inmates. Some death-penalty supporters, noting that more than two-thirds of Americans back capital punishment, say the research validates the views of a relatively silent majority.

And victims' rights groups that have felt excluded from the debate over executions say the professors give them moral support.

"It's been easy for the media to dismiss [death-penalty supporters] as just a rabble that wants to 'hang 'em all,'" says Dudley Sharp, resource director for Justice For All, a victims' rights group in Houston. "Now we've got research, respectability—things that have always been conceded to the other side. It's more of a real debate."

A study last year by researchers at Emory University in Atlanta examined the nearly 6,000 death sentences imposed in the USA from 1977 through 1996. The authors compared changes in murder rates in 3,000 U.S. counties to the likelihood of being executed for murder in that county. They found that murder rates declined in counties where capital punishment was imposed. The researchers said a statistical formula suggested that each execution saved the lives of 18 potential victims.

Recent studies at the University of Houston and at the University of Colorado at Denver had similar findings. Blecker, who is researching deterrence, says they square with what he found in interviews with 60 killers. "They are cognizant of whether they are operating in a death-penalty state before they pull the trigger," he says. "They're operating in the real world, not the realm of political theory."

To [Marquette University professor John] McAdams, the debate over deterrence is unnecessary. "If you execute a murderer and it stops other murders, you've saved innocent lives," he says. "And if it doesn't, you've executed a murderer. Where's the problem?"

Academics who back executions are gaining some acceptance. Senate Republicans countered [an anti–death penalty] bill by citing research from pro-death penalty academics. The bill was approved by the Judiciary Committee but is stalled in the Senate.

Meanwhile, Blecker says he's getting asked to more academic conferences on the death penalty—usually as the only voice in favor. "'A lion in a den of Daniels' is one way I've been introduced," he says.

—Richard Willing

## A WAR OF STATISTICS

Death penalty opponents criticize studies that show that capital punishment deters future murderers. They point out many flaws in the researchers' data collection and methods of analysis. They also say that statistical studies can never measure all the factors that influence individual acts of murder. What about homicides that result from emotional outbursts, for example? Does it make sense that a person in a murderous rage would stop to think about his or her chances of being executed? What about a person who is high on drugs? Will he or she stop to consider the consequences of committing murder?

Many factors influence murder rates, critics of the studies say. These factors include economic conditions, law-enforcement practices, and gun laws—all of which change over time. Critics of the deterrence studies say it's impossible to show that a rising or falling murder rate, by itself, is specifically linked to capital punishment. Too many other factors come into play.

USA TODAY Snapshots®

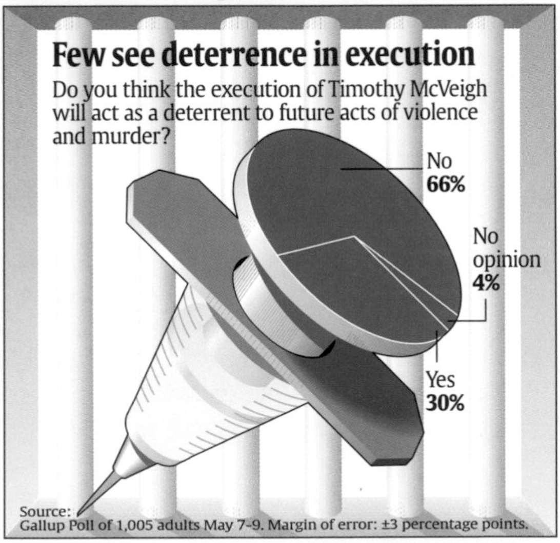
Few see deterrence in execution
Do you think the execution of Timothy McVeigh will act as a deterrent to future acts of violence and murder?
No 66%
No opinion 4%
Yes 30%
Source: Gallup Poll of 1,005 adults May 7-9. Margin of error: ±3 percentage points.

By Lori Joseph and Marcy E. Mullins, USA TODAY, 2001

Critics also point to the very few death sentences imposed each year (111 in 2008) versus the vast number of murders (about 16,000) committed each year in the United States. These figures show that a person's chances of receiving the death penalty for murder are extremely low—far less than 1 percent. With commuted and overturned sentences, the odds of a murderer actually being executed are even smaller. With such slim odds of execution, opponents of the death penalty suggest, it is highly unlikely that capital punishment will deter anyone from committing murder.

Some people even argue that capital punishment might increase rather than decrease future murders. They say that a nation that punishes people with death encourages violence, leading to an increase in murder and other violence. Another argument suggests that for some people, the risk of being put to death for murder may even heighten their excitement in doing it.

Death penalty opponents offer statistics and studies of their own. They note that most of the states that don't use the death penalty have murder rates well below the national average. The northeastern states, which carry out fewer than 1 percent of all executions, have the nation's lowest murder rate. On the flip side, the southern states, which carry out more than 80 percent of the nation's executions, have the nation's highest murder rate. Death penalty opponents point out that, under the deterrence argument, the results should be the opposite.

Most people on the front lines of crime and punishment say that the death penalty does not deter future crime. In a 1995 poll of 386 police chiefs across the United States, 67 percent said they believed the death penalty was not a deterrent to criminals. The chiefs noted that reducing drug abuse, putting more cops on the streets, imposing longer prison sentences to keep criminals off the streets, streamlining court cases, and improving job opportunities in poor neighborhoods were much more likely to reduce violent crime than was the death penalty.

But death penalty advocates say that regardless of deterrence, executing convicted murderers is a good idea.

# Weighing the Costs

Money is a big part of the death penalty debate. Death penalty supporters object to the expenses involved in locking up prisoners for life. They say that taxpayers do not want to support killers for years and years. They also note that as life in prison without parole (LWOP) prisoners age and grow sick, the cost of caring for their medical needs soars.

*Above:* Death row at Huntsville Prison in Texas

It seems logical that shortening the life of a murderer would save taxpayers money. But many studies show that it is actually two or three times more expensive to execute a prisoner than to keep him or her locked up for life. The additional expense stems from extra trial costs, the lengthy appeals process, and the extra security required for prisoners on death row. Recent studies reveal:

- In Tennessee, the average death penalty trial costs almost 50 percent more than the average trial involving life in prison.
- It cost the U.S. government more than $13 million to convict and execute Oklahoma City bomber Timothy McVeigh.
- The typical death penalty murder case in Kansas costs $1.26 million, compared to $740,000 for the typical non-death penalty murder case. These figures include the cost of keeping an inmate on death row or in prison for life.
- Florida would save $51 million each year by punishing murderers with LWOP instead of death, according to a 2000 study.
- California could save up to $100 million a year by abolishing the death penalty, according to a 2008 report.

Death penalty supporters take issue with these statistics. They argue that death penalty opponents overlook some important data, such as the high costs of keeping prisoners locked up for life and LWOP appeals. Over time, they argue, the typical LWOP case costs $1.2 to $2.6 million more than the typical death penalty case.

John McAdams, a political scientist at Marquette University in Wisconsin, provides this explanation:

> If we execute murderers, and there is, in fact, no deterrent effect, we have killed a bunch of murderers. If we fail to execute murderers, and doing so would have deterred other murderers, we have allowed the killing of a bunch of innocent victims. I would much rather risk the former [first option]. This, to me, is not a tough call.

## REPEAT KILLERS

Related to the question of deterrence is recidivism—a person's relapse, or return to criminal behavior, after serving time in prison. Death penalty supporters note that murderers released from U.S. jails and prisons sometimes kill again. One sure way to avoid this situation is to execute murderers so they can't kill anyone else.

Just having a murderer locked up behind bars is no guarantee that he or she won't kill again, death penalty supporters say. On numerous occasions, death row inmates have killed prison guards, other prison staff, and other inmates. Convicted killer Robert Lynn Pruett was already

> **"Some claim life without parole is an adequate substitute [for the death penalty]. What they fail to note are the people, both inside and outside prison, who die at the hands of convicted murderers."**
>
> **—JOSHUA MARQUIS,**
> PROSECUTING ATTORNEY, 2005

USA TODAY Snapshots®

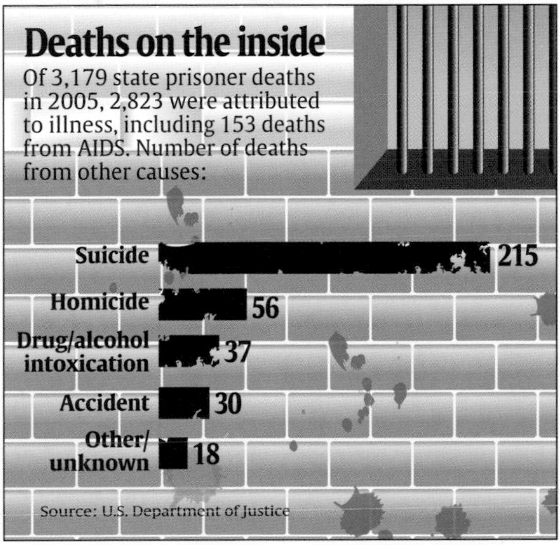
Deaths on the inside
Of 3,179 state prisoner deaths in 2005, 2,823 were attributed to illness, including 153 deaths from AIDS. Number of deaths from other causes:
Suicide
215
Homicide
56
Drug/alcohol intoxication
37
Accident
30
Other/ unknown
18
Source: U.S. Department of Justice

By David Stuckey and Alejandro Gonzalez, USA TODAY, 2007

serving a life sentence in Texas when he used a makeshift weapon to kill guard Daniel Nagle in 1999. Cuhuatemoc Peraita, convicted of murdering three coworkers during a 1994 robbery, was locked up for life without parole in Alabama. In 1999 Peraita and a fellow inmate used a prison-made knife to murder a third inmate. Both Pruett and Peraita got death sentences after committing these additional murders.

Dora Larson, whose ten-year-old daughter was kidnapped, raped, and strangled, supported the death penalty for her daughter's killer—in part to protect society. She explained, "[Families'] biggest fear is that some day, our child or loved one's killer will be released. And we know we never, ever get our loved one back. But we want these people off the streets so that others might be safe. To many of us, justice means we never have to worry that our killer will ever kill again."

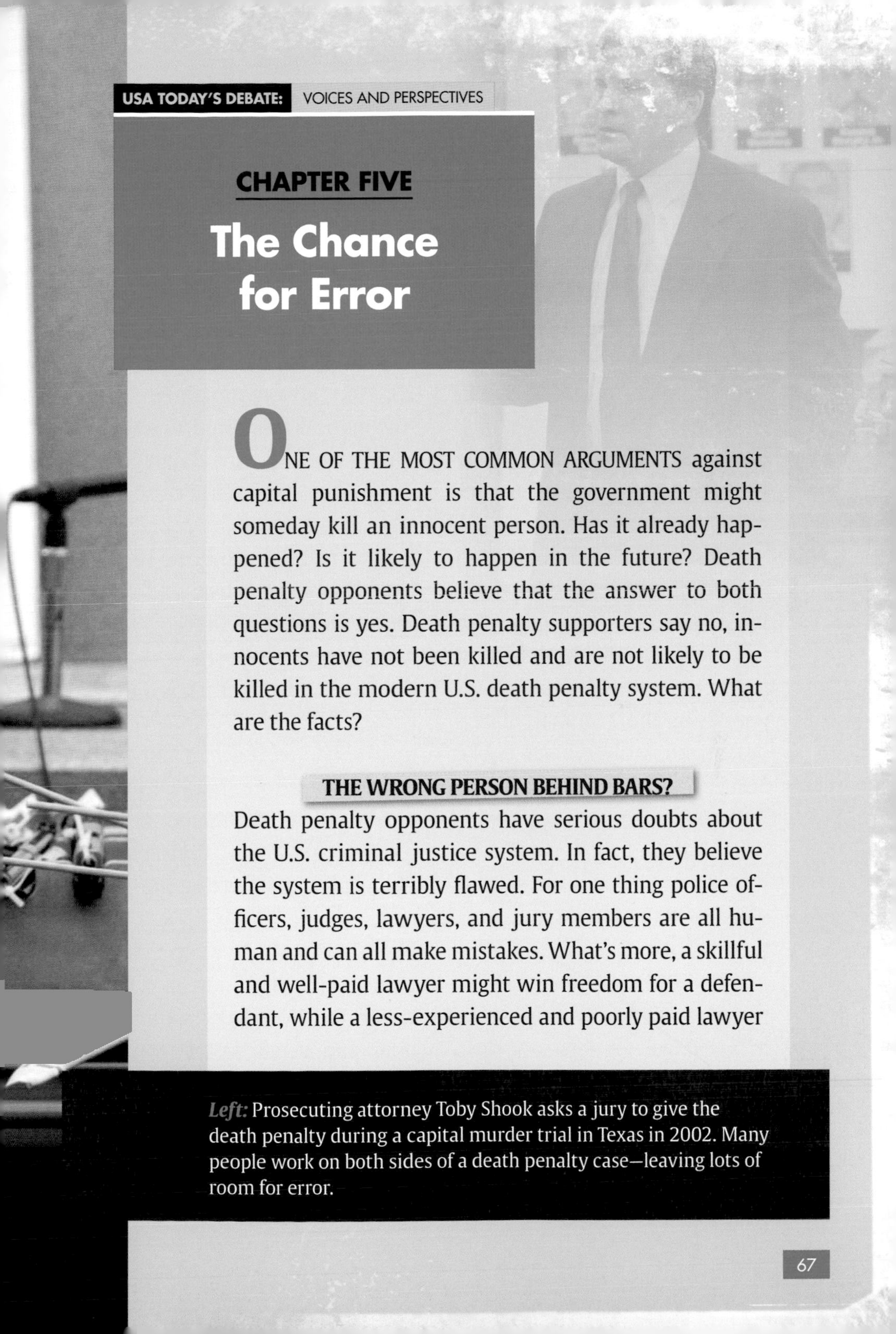

## CHAPTER FIVE

# The Chance for Error

ONE OF THE MOST COMMON ARGUMENTS against capital punishment is that the government might someday kill an innocent person. Has it already happened? Is it likely to happen in the future? Death penalty opponents believe that the answer to both questions is yes. Death penalty supporters say no, innocents have not been killed and are not likely to be killed in the modern U.S. death penalty system. What are the facts?

### THE WRONG PERSON BEHIND BARS?

Death penalty opponents have serious doubts about the U.S. criminal justice system. In fact, they believe the system is terribly flawed. For one thing police officers, judges, lawyers, and jury members are all human and can all make mistakes. What's more, a skillful and well-paid lawyer might win freedom for a defendant, while a less-experienced and poorly paid lawyer

*Left:* Prosecuting attorney Toby Shook asks a jury to give the death penalty during a capital murder trial in Texas in 2002. Many people work on both sides of a death penalty case—leaving lots of room for error.

might lose the same case. One jury might find a defendant innocent, while a different jury might convict that person on the exact same charge. Laboratories can make mistakes when testing blood and other body fluids from a crime scene. When someone's life is on the line, death penalty opponents ask, How can we trust a system that is anything but perfect?

Most people working in the U.S. criminal justice system are fair and honest. They follow the law and try to protect citizens' rights. But it's also true that people in the criminal justice system don't always act nobly. Sometimes prosecutors cut corners to win cases. They sometimes rely on faulty evidence or hide important evidence from defense attorneys. Sometimes they allow jailhouse informants—"jailhouse snitches"—to testify against other prisoners in exchange for leniency (less severe judgments) in their own cases. But jailhouse snitches are famous for telling lies. In the worst cases, police officers might brutalize suspects to get false confessions. This sort of behavior is itself criminal. It can also result in the conviction of an innocent person.

The case of Ray Krone demonstrates how the system can go terribly wrong. On December 29, 1991, a woman named Kim Ancona was found murdered in a bar in Phoenix, Arizona, where she worked. She had been sexually assaulted and stabbed to death. The evidence at the scene included blood, saliva, and bite marks on Ancona's body.

A friend of Ancona told police that a customer named Ray Krone had helped Ancona close up the bar on the night of the murder. Police questioned Krone and made an impression of his teeth in a piece of Styrofoam. Then police claimed that the bite marks on the Styrofoam and the bite marks on the victim's body were a match. They charged Krone with murder, kidnapping, and sexual assault. Krone claimed to be innocent. He said he had been home asleep at the time of the murder.

The case went badly for Krone. He was found guilty and

sentenced to death. He appealed his case and won a new trial in 1996, but again a jury found him guilty. Meanwhile, the time for Krone's execution drew closer.

Fortunately for Ray Krone, new technology entered the criminal justice system in the 1990s. This technology was DNA testing, which involves analyzing genetic material from the human body. In 2002 DNA testing proved that neither the blood nor the saliva at the crime scene belonged to Ray Krone. The test also enabled investigators to identify the real killer, Kenneth Phillips, who received a long prison sentence for the crime. After ten years on death row, Ray Krone left prison on April 8, 2002. He had lost ten years of freedom and nearly lost his life.

*Above:* Ray Krone sits outside his mother's home in Pennsylvania. He was exonerated (cleared) of a murder he did not commit after spending ten years on death row.

# DNA Evidence

DNA, or deoxyribonucleic acid, is genetic material found inside the cells of all living things. In human beings, DNA governs eye color, hair color, size, and many other physical traits. Except in the case of identical twins, each person's DNA is different.

Blood, saliva, sweat, hair, skin, and other biological materials all contain DNA. Often, these materials are left behind at crime scenes. Criminal investigators can test DNA from a crime scene *(right)* and compare it to DNA from a suspect. If the DNA matches, investigators have proof that the suspect was at the crime scene. Police departments started using DNA testing to identify suspects in the late 1980s.

In addition to helping investigators find and convict criminals, DNA can also help prove someone's innocence. For instance, DNA testing showed that Ray Krone's blood and saliva did not match the blood and saliva at the scene of Kim Ancona's murder. DNA testing also led police to the real killer in that case.

DNA testing can be critical in death penalty cases, since juries want to know for certain that they're convicting the right person for a crime. But DNA testing is not foolproof. Lab workers sometimes make mistakes, DNA samples can be contaminated, and test results can be mixed up or misread. Nevertheless, continued and improved use of DNA testing promises to reduce the risk that an innocent person will face execution.

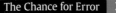

USA TODAY Snapshots®

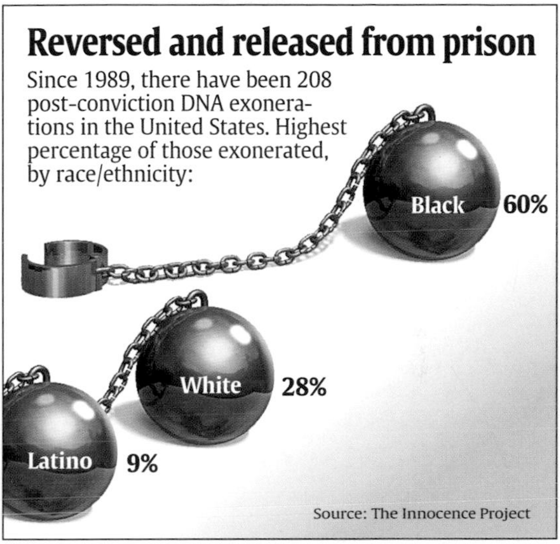

Reversed and released from prison
Since 1989, there have been 208 post-conviction DNA exonerations in the United States. Highest percentage of those exonerated, by race/ethnicity:
Black 60%
White 28%
Latino 9%
Source: The Innocence Project


By David Stuckey and Karl Gelles, USA TODAY, 2007

The Death Penalty Information Center (DPIC) is a Washington, D.C.–based organization that provides information on the death penalty to the media and public. According to the DPIC, since 1973 more than 130 other Americans have been released from death row after a court overturned their convictions. Of this group, at least thirty-four were proven to be "actually innocent"—meaning they definitely had not committed the crime with which they had been charged. Those in the remaining group were considered "legally innocent." Legal innocence means the defendants should not have been convicted in the first place, perhaps because of insufficient evidence or errors by the police or prosecution.

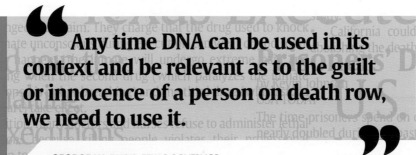

**"Any time DNA can be used in its context and be relevant as to the guilt or innocence of a person on death row, we need to use it."**

—**GEORGE W. BUSH,** TEXAS GOVERNOR
**USA TODAY · JUNE 2, 2000**

News
SECTION A

October 13, 2004

# Wrongly convicted walk away with scars

From the Pages of USA TODAY

EVEN AFTER HIS PARDON, they called Kirk Bloodworth a child killer.

After nearly nine years in prison, Bloodworth walked away in 1993 when DNA tests showed he was wrongly convicted of raping and murdering a 9-year-old girl. He was now a free man, the first death row prisoner exonerated because of DNA evidence.

But his trials weren't over.

Employers were leery of hiring someone who'd spent so long in jail. When he landed a job at a tool company, co-workers left newspaper clippings about the crime at his workstation. Suspicions followed him like a shadow. Bloodworth got a door-to-door fundraising job, but a homeowner recognized him and began yelling "child killer" at him as Bloodworth stood on the front stoop.

"I never got a fair shake," says Bloodworth, 44, of Cambridge, Maryland, who works as a crab fisherman on his boat, *Freedom*, and is a program officer with The Justice Project, a group that campaigns for criminal justice reform. "It's hard to come back to this world and be accepted after you've been in prison so long, especially to the workplace. That's very sad."

With the advent of DNA testing, more prisoners are being freed after wrongful convictions. The pace of exonerations has jumped sharply, from about 12 a year

*Above:* Kirk Bloodworth testifies before a committee about being an innocent person on death row.

through the early 1990s to an average of 43 a year since 2000, according to a study by the University of Michigan. There have been at least 328 exonerations since 1989, and about half of those since 1999 were based on DNA evidence. There are at least 41 Innocence Projects in 31 states providing legal assistance to inmates.

But as the number of exonerees grows, concerns are mounting about the difficulties these former prisoners experience in finding employment once they're free. While prison parolees typically get free job placement assistance, temporary housing and counseling, the exonerated often are released into an employment no-man's land.

They get scant help finding work. They have resume gaps from spending years in prison. The average time from conviction to exoneration is more than 11 years, according to the University of Michigan study. They often get little more than a new overcoat or bus money.

Only 18 states, the federal government and Washington, D.C., have laws for compensating [providing money to] the exonerated. Compensation can take years to get, and the laws often aren't used by exonerees because they may need an official pardon or a court must declare them innocent.

Compensation amounts can vary widely. Some states, such as West Virginia, have no cap on the amount that can be received; others, such as Maine, set a maximum of $300,000.

Employers are leery of hiring convicts who may have been wrongfully convicted. Job skills are so obsolete [out of date] that some exonerees have never sent an e-mail or typed on a computer.

A large number of these men—more than 95% are men, according to the Michigan study—grapple with emotional problems. Some have narrowly escaped execution on death row. Others have been assaulted by other inmates or kept in isolation. Many are angry. Some resort to crime after their release.

"Innocent people do some of the hardest time. They never reconcile themselves to why they're in prison. They feel their lives have been taken away," says Justin Brooks, executive director of the Innocence Project chapter at California Western School of Law in San Diego. "We expect them to just start functioning in the workforce. But there's a stigma to having been incarcerated [imprisoned]."

—Stephanie Armour

## AN INNOCENT MAN EXECUTED?

Although he lost ten years of his life in prison, Ray Krone was still lucky not to be executed. But has the system ever failed completely? Has an innocent person ever been executed? Some people say yes. "There is no question in my mind . . . that we certainly have in the past executed those people who either didn't fit the criteria for execution in the State of Florida or who, in fact, were factually not guilty of the crime for which they have been executed," states Gerald Kogan, who has worked as a prosecutor, defense attorney, and judge in Florida.

One uncertain case involves a man named Cameron Willingham. In 1991 Willingham's Texas home burned to the ground. The fire killed Willingham's three daughters. Willingham claimed the fire was accidental, but prosecutors said that Willingham had deliberately started the fire. They charged him with murder. Willingham was found guilty and sentenced to death. He lived on death row for thirteen years.

Shortly before Willingham's scheduled execution, an arson expert, Gerald Hurst, got

**"Evidence indicates that . . . innocent people are sentenced to death with materially greater frequency than was previously supposed and . . . proof of their innocence often does not emerge until long after their convictions."**

—**JED RAKOFF,** U.S. DISTRICT JUDGE, 2002

USA TODAY · JULY 2, 2002

involved in the case. He concluded that the original arson investigators had used faulty methods in proving that Willingham had set the fire. In fact, Hurst said, "There's nothing to suggest to any reasonable arson investigator that this was an arson fire. It was just a fire."

Willingham's attorney asked the Texas Court of Criminal Appeals and Texas governor Rick Perry to consider Hurst's report and to delay the execution. But the court and the governor agreed with the original guilty verdict. Willingham died by lethal injection on February 17, 2004. Dorinda Brokofsky, a juror who had originally voted to convict Willingham, was despondent when she learned of the new evidence. "Now I will have to live with this for the rest of my life," she said. "Maybe this man was innocent."

Death penalty opponents say that the only way to completely ensure that an innocent person won't be executed is to abolish capital punishment altogether. What do death penalty supporters say?

## THE OTHER SIDE OF INNOCENCE

Death penalty supporters defend the U.S. criminal justice system as fair and careful. They say innocent people are extremely unlikely to end up on death row. The appeals system is designed to prevent mistakes, and it works, they say. Robert Pambianco, an attorney from Washington, D.C., writes, "While imperfect, the system bends over backward to ensure the guilt of those executed, and people can be more certain about capital punishment than most else in life." He continues, "Judges love to overturn death sentences. Appeals courts make these decisions all the time, not because the system is flawed but because the system is super cautious about executions. As it should be."

Paul Valone, a columnist for the *Charlotte Observer* in North Carolina, agrees. Valone once served as a juror in a murder trial. He reports, "The weeks I spent being scrutinized as a prospective juror, and instructed in the law as foreman [leader] of

## The Innocence Project

In 1992 lawyers Barry Scheck and Peter Neufeld started an organization called the Innocence Project. The project tests DNA evidence from old criminal cases that were carried out without DNA testing. In many cases, the new tests find that people have been imprisoned for crimes they didn't commit. Innocence Project lawyers have reopened hundreds of old cases and retried them using new DNA tests. This work has resulted in the release of more than 215 wrongly convicted prisoners. Sixteen of them had been on death row.

the jury in a murder case, impressed me that the process is anything but 'arbitrary.'" When President George W. Bush was governor of Texas from 1994 to 2000, he signed off on 152 executions. "I take every death penalty case seriously and review each case carefully," Bush stated. "Each case is major because each case is life or death."

Death penalty supporters are quick to attack the Death Penalty Information Center's list of more than 130 "innocents" released from death row since 1973. They stress that most people on the list were found to be "legally innocent"—that is, their convictions were overturned for technical reasons, such as judge or prosecutor error, not because their "actual innocence" was proven. When tallying innocents on death row, death penalty supporters say, the "legally innocent" group must be taken out of the equation. Joshua K. Marquis, an attorney in western Oregon, remarks, "Most of the people freed from death row are anything but innocent, and police and prosecutors almost always do get the right person."

Is the risk of an innocent person being executed justification for abolishing the death penalty altogether? Death penalty supporters say no. After all, innocent people might also end up in prison for life. Should we also shut down the prison system because it, too, is flawed? Many people will die each year on U.S. highways, they say. Should we shut the highways down too? The solution, death penalty supporters say, is improving the death penalty system, not shutting it down. Marquis continues, "There are indeed stories of people wrongfully sent to prison and even death row, but they are so few and the situation so easily remedied that they are hardly the basis for abolishing the ultimate punishment for the worst of murderers."

D.R. # 999141

Name: Napoleon Beazley

Age: 18 (when rec'd)

DOB: 08/05/76

Received: 03/21/95

Date of Offense: 04/19/94

County: Smith

Race: Black

Height:

Age at time of offense: 17

Hair: Black

Eyes: Brown

Weight:

State: Texas

Native County: Houston

Education Level: 12 years

Prior Occupation: Laborer

**Prior Prison Record:**

None

**Summary:**

Convicted in the car jacking murder of 63-year-old John E. Luttig of Tyler. Luttig, driving Mercedes Benz, had pulled into the driveway of his home at 120 South College when approached by Beazley and shot in the head with a .45-caliber pistol. Beazley and two accon who had followed Luttig home, fled his vehicle.

**Co-Defendants:**

Donald Coleman and Cedric Coleman. Charges of capital murder and aggravated robb pending.

**Race of Victim(s):**

White male

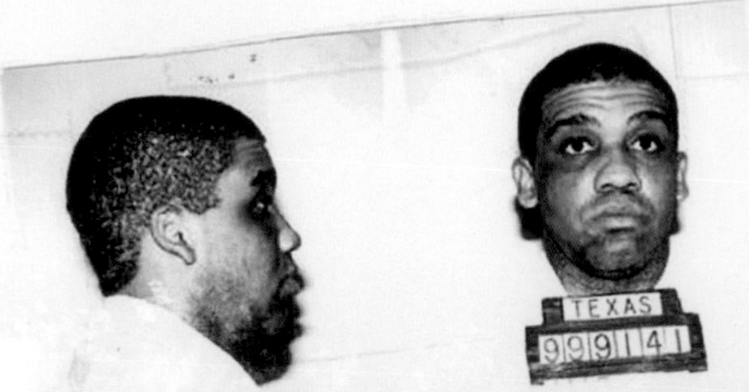

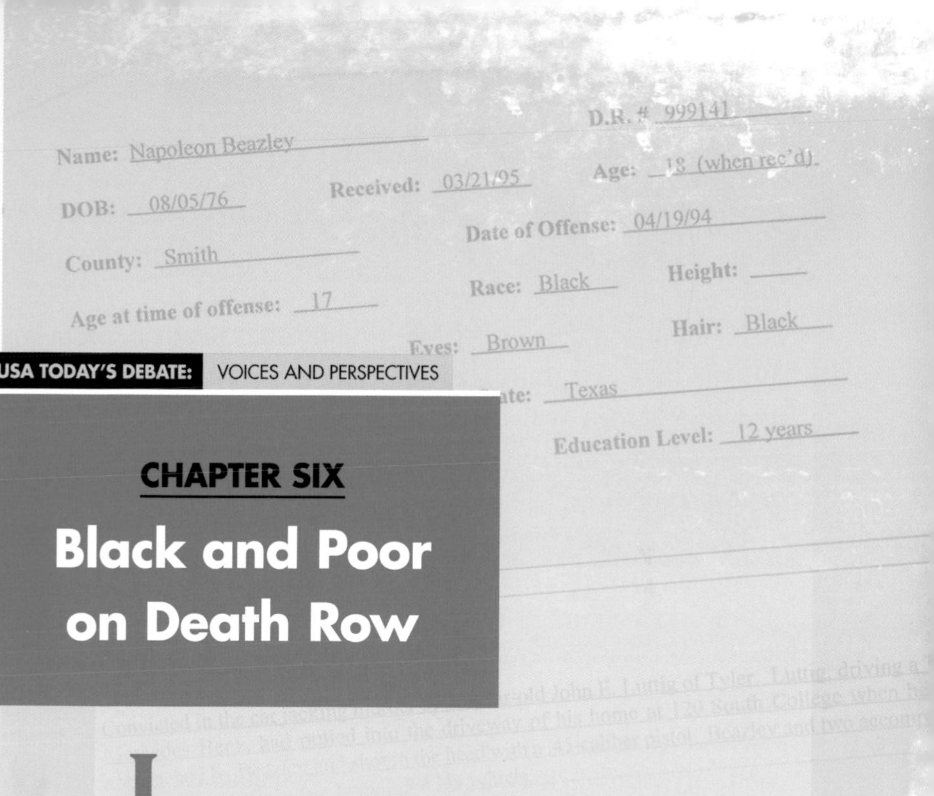
D.R. # 999141

Name: Napoleon Beazley

DOB: 08/05/76 Received: 03/21/95 Age: 18 (when rec'd)

County: Smith Date of Offense: 04/19/94

Age at time of offense: 17 Race: Black Height:

Eyes: Brown Hair: Black

...ate: Texas

Education Level: 12 years



## CHAPTER SIX

# Black and Poor on Death Row

IN 1994 NAPOLEON BEAZLEY, A YOUNG AFRICAN American man, told friends that he wanted to know what it felt like to kill somebody. Later that day, he found out. He shot and killed John Luttig of Tyler, Texas. In the wake of the crime, the public clamored for the death penalty. Luttig was a rich white businessman and the father of a prominent federal judge. He was considered an upstanding citizen of Tyler. Townspeople expected the ultimate punishment for Luttig's killer. The prosecutor pursued the death penalty.

But two years later, when two young white men in Tyler shot Ivan Holland, a homeless African American man, the prosecutor didn't ask for the death penalty.

*Left:* This police report was written up the night Napoleon Beazley was arrested on suspicion of capital murder and aggravated robbery.

Instead, he cut a deal with the killers. In exchange for a guilty plea, one killer got forty-five years in prison for his crime and the other got thirty-seven years. Both men will be eligible for parole after serving half their sentences.

Was John Luttig's life worth more than Ivan Holland's? Why did the prosecutors in Tyler aggressively pursue the death penalty when a black man killed a rich white man but pass on the death penalty when two white men killed a poor black man?

Questions of race loom large in death penalty debates. Opponents charge that the judicial system is biased against African Americans and other minorities, and biased against the poor in general. Supporters say the system is color-blind and that it treats everyone—rich and poor—fairly and equally. Each side uses statistics and studies to support its case.

## A RACIST SYSTEM?

"The [death penalty] system has proved itself to be . . . at times, a very racist system," wrote former Illinois governor George Ryan, who emptied his state's death row in 2003. He and other death penalty critics argue that an African American person charged with murder is much more likely to end up on death row than a white person charged with murder—especially if the victim is white.

Racial bias is prevalent in U.S. society, and death penalty opponents say it's prevalent in the judicial system, too—from law enforcement to prosecution to jury selection to sentencing. The Reverend Joseph Lowery, former president of the Southern Christian Leadership Conference (a group that works for racial equality), sees the death penalty as a continuation of long-standing racial discrimination in the United States. He writes, "By reserving the penalty of death for black defendants, or for the poor, or for those convicted of killing white persons, we perpetrate the ugly legacy of slavery—teaching our children that some lives are inherently less precious than others."

# Demographic Breakdowns for Executions
## 1977–2007

**Gender of Defendants Executed 1977–2007**

| | |
|---|---|
| Female | 11 (1.1%) |
| Male | 1,088 (99%) |

**Race of Defendants Executed 1977–2007**

| | |
|---|---|
| White | 626 (56.96%) |
| Black | 376 (34.21%) |
| Latino | 75 (6.82%) |
| Native American | 15 (1.36%) |
| Asian | 7 (0.64%) |

**Gender of Victims 1977–2007**

| | |
|---|---|
| Female | 806 (49.27%) |
| Male | 830 (50.73%) |

**Race of Victims 1977–2007**

| | |
|---|---|
| White | 1,295 (79.16%) |
| Black | 226 (13.81%) |
| Latino | 81 (4.95%) |
| Native American | 5 (0.31%) |
| Asian | 29 (1.77%) |

In one famous study, law professor David Baldus examined the Chattahoochee Judicial District in Georgia to see how racial bias affected death-penalty decisions there. Baldus reviewed all murder cases in the district from 1973 to 1990. After the murder of a white person, Baldus noted, prosecutors routinely met with the victim's family members and discussed whether or not to seek the death penalty. But during the same period, prosecutors rarely met with families of black murder victims to discuss the death penalty. As a result, although 65 percent of the district's homicide victims were black, 85 percent of death penalty cases involved white murder victims.

A 2006 study from South Carolina had similar findings. In that state, prosecutors are three times more likely to seek the death penalty in cases with white murder victims than those with black murder victims, and prosecutors are three and a half times more likely to seek the death penalty when a black defendant has killed a white victim than all other victim/defendant combinations put together.

Death penalty opponents say that racism also reigns in jury selection. For example, statistics show that prosecutors in death penalty cases reject prospective African American jurors in far greater numbers than prospective white jurors. In Philadelphia, Pennsylvania, assistant district attorney (prosecutor) Jack McMahon once instructed new prosecutors to try to keep blacks off juries because "blacks from low-income areas are less likely to convict. Young black women are very bad [at convicting]."

In death-penalty states, most U.S. prosecutors (about 98 percent) are white. Most judges are white as well. So, in many situations, white prosecutors, white judges, and white juries decide the fate of black defendants who have killed white victims. In theory, the judicial system should still be fair. But racism can poison the process. Death-penalty opponents note numerous examples

*Above:* Often, all-white or mostly white juries decide the fate of African American defendants in death penalty cases.

of white judges, prosecutors, jurors, and even defense attorneys using racial slurs in court or publically discussing their racial prejudices. For example, a Missouri judge—Earl Blackwell—was presiding over a death penalty case against a black defendant in 1991. During the case, he switched his political allegiance from the Democratic Party to the Republican Party. In a press release explaining the switch, he made his racial biases loud and clear. The Democratic Party "places far too much emphasis on representing minorities . . . people who don't want to work, and people with a skin that's any color but white," he said.

The late Supreme Court justice Thurgood Marshall, an African American, believed the death penalty system was riddled with bias. In 1990 he stated, "When in *Gregg v. Georgia* the Supreme Court gave its seal of approval to capital punishment, this endorsement was premised [based] on the promise that capital punishment would be administered with fairness and justice. Instead, the promise has become a cruel and empty mockery. If not remedied, the scandalous state of our present system of capital punishment will cast a pall of shame over our society for years to come. We cannot let it continue."

## NOT EVERYONE AGREES

Death penalty supporters deny that the system is racist. They note that death penalty opponents often cite out-of-date statistics to make their case. Studies that include data from the late 1970s, for instance, do not give an accurate picture of the modern death-penalty system. Supporters say that system is largely free from racial bias.

The U.S. Justice Department examined the question of racism in the federal death penalty system in 2001. In its study, the department found no evidence of discrimination toward minorities. In fact, the study found that the U.S. attorney general pursued the death penalty more often for white defendants than for African Americans and other minorities. Before Governor Ryan called off executions in Illinois in 2000, the state's convicted white murderers were sentenced to death two and a half times more often than African American murderers.

It's true that blacks are disproportionately represented on death row: African Americans make up just 12 percent of the U.S. population but account for about 42 percent of death row inmates. But death penalty supporters say a racist justice system is not to blame. They say that, compared to their numbers in the population (12 percent), blacks simply commit more murders than whites. To take a sample year, in 2004 African Americans committed approximately 35 percent of murders in the United States, according to the Federal Bureau of Investigation.

As for the victim's race—the fact that murderers (black or white) are more likely to get the death penalty for killing a white person than for killing a black person—death penalty supporters offer this explanation. They say whites are more likely to be victims of capital murders—that is, murders that make the killer eligible for the death penalty.

USA TODAY
News
SECTION A
February 8, 2005

# To Prejean, death penalty system is guilty as sin

From the Pages of USA TODAY

During the summers of the 5½ years it took Sister Helen Prejean to write *The Death of Innocents: An Eyewitness Account of Wrongful Executions*, she sought refuge in a place called Prayer Lodge on the Northern Cheyenne Reservation in Montana.

*The Death of Innocents* is about the death penalty and justice, a subject she also visited in *Dead Man Walking*, her first book, which was published in 1993. Two years later, it became the basis for a major film with the same title. Susan Sarandon, who played Prejean in the movie, won an Oscar.

Prejean, a nun with the Sisters of St. Joseph of Medaille in New Orleans, joined the convent at 18 and taught English and religion for 11 years, four in the classroom and seven in adult education. It was in the 1980s that she began working with prisoners on death row.

The judicial system, she writes, is filled with flaws, citing the "astonishing admissions of errors by state and federal courts forced to free 117 people from death row since 1973." She points out the disparity in meting [handing] out the death penalty in the 38 states where it is allowed—especially in the South.

Race, she says, is one factor: "Overwhelmingly, when people are selected for the death penalty, it is because they killed a white person."

Another factor, she says, is politics: Winning the death penalty is a way to further a legal career.

Poverty, too, plays a role. Prejean, in her work in the St. Thomas Housing Project in New Orleans, recalls an axiom [saying] from there: "Capital punishment means 'Them without the capital get the punishment.'"

"The Supreme Court can tinker with the death penalty guidelines all it wants," she writes, "but patterns of implementation clearly show that who is killed and who is spared is determined largely by local culture—'our way of doing things'—and not by law."

—Jacqueline Blais

For instance, whites are more likely to be killed by serial killers, during robberies, or during sexual assaults—all situations that make a murderer eligible for the death penalty. African Americans are more likely to be victims of noncapital murders, such as those that occur during domestic disputes. Noncapital murders are not punishable by death.

Another explanation offered by death penalty supporters concerns the urban/rural split in the United States. Americans in rural areas tend to support the death penalty more than urban dwellers. In Illinois, for instance, a murderer is five times more likely to get the death penalty in a rural area than in the big city of Chicago. Since more whites than African Americans live in rural areas, it makes sense that murder victims in rural areas tend to be white too. And pro–death penalty rural communities are more likely to want the death penalty for the victims' murderers whether they are black or white.

## CUT-RATE JUSTICE?

A common death rowing saying is: "Them that has the capital don't get the punishment." *Capital* is another word for "money." In other words, rich people don't end up on death row. The saying appears to make sense. After all, poor people can't afford skillful, high-priced defense attorneys to fight on their behalf. Without good attorneys, they are more likely to lose a death penalty case in court. Sister Helen Prejean noted that in 1997, 99 percent of the 3,100 Americans on death row were poor. She explains,

> When people of color are killed in the inner city, when homeless people are killed, when the "nobodies" are killed, district attorneys do not seek to avenge their deaths. Black, Hispanic, or poor families who have a loved one murdered not only don't expect the district attorney's office to pursue the death penalty—which of course is both costly and time consuming—but are surprised when the case is prosecuted at all.

A few murder defendants can afford high-powered attorneys. When football legend O. J. Simpson went on trial for murder in 1995, he was able to hire a "dream team" of expensive lawyers. Paid millions of dollars for its work, the dream team helped earn Simpson a not-guilty verdict.

But most murder defendants—about nine out of ten in death penalty cases—rely on public (government-appointed) attorneys to defend them. Funding for these attorneys varies by state. In some states, especially in the South, government-appointed attorneys are overworked and underpaid. They don't have big budgets and large staffs to help them, as many prosecuting attorneys do. Bryan Stevenson, director of the Equal Justice Initiative of Alabama, noted that in 2002, 80 percent of Alabama's death row inmates were represented by attorneys whose pay was capped by state law at one thousand dollars

Double murder defendant O. J. Simpson *(seated, center)* is surrounded by his high-powered and high-priced defense team: *(clockwise from left)* Johnnie Cochran, Peter Neufeld, Robert Shapiro, Robert Kardashian, and Robert Blasier.

per case. In Illinois two defense attorneys handled 103 cases in one year for a total fee of thirty thousand dollars. That comes out to less than three hundred dollars per case. By contrast, private attorneys can earn millions of dollars per year to represent their clients.

When their minimal state pay runs out, some public defense attorneys choose to keep working without pay, seeing their clients through many years of appeals for free. They do so because they believe that all citizens have the right to have legal representation. Some nonprofit law firms, such as the Capital Appeals Project in New Orleans, Louisiana, also represent death row inmates for free.

But many defense attorneys avoid taking government jobs altogether because the pay is so low. Often, government-appointed attorneys are fresh out of law school and lack experience. And a few defense lawyers, such as one who took naps during a murder trial, probably shouldn't be practicing law at all. A 2001 study in Washington State revealed some alarming facts about government-appointed defense attorneys. The study showed that 20 percent of attorneys who represented capital defendants in Washington were later disbarred (banned from practicing law),

> **"People who are well represented at trial do not get the death penalty. I have yet to see a death case among the dozens coming to the Supreme Court on eve-of-execution stay applications in which the defendant was well represented at trial."**
>
> —RUTH BADER GINSBURG, SUPREME COURT JUSTICE, 2001

> **"The state [Kentucky] funded Department of Public Advocacy provides consistently superior legal representation to the state's indigent [poor] defendants, and this is particularly true for those subject to the death penalty."**
>
> **—GEORGE MOORE, PRESIDENT,**
> KENTUCKY ATTORNEY'S ASSOCIATION, 2000s

temporarily suspended from practicing law, or arrested.

Not everyone agrees that the death penalty discriminates against the poor. Joshua Marquis notes that in 2001 the state of Oregon spent $75 million to defend those who couldn't afford to pay for a lawyer. During the same year, Oregon spent less than $50 million to prosecute cases.

George Moore, president of Kentucky's attorney's association, argues that Kentucky gives top-level representation to death penalty defendants. "The defendant facing the death penalty is provided not one, but two, attorneys at the trial level," Moore told a group of state lawmakers. "Additional . . . personnel are at the beck and call of the assigned counsel [lawyers]. . . . An equally skilled level of representation is then in place for the exhaustive appeals."

Death penalty supporters say that charges of inadequate legal representation, like charges of racism, are based on outdated statistics and stories. They note that nearly all death penalty states have recently raised standards for government-appointed defense attorneys and have passed other reforms to ensure that death row defendants get skilled representation.

SIMMONS C
990111
09 30 03
MO DOC

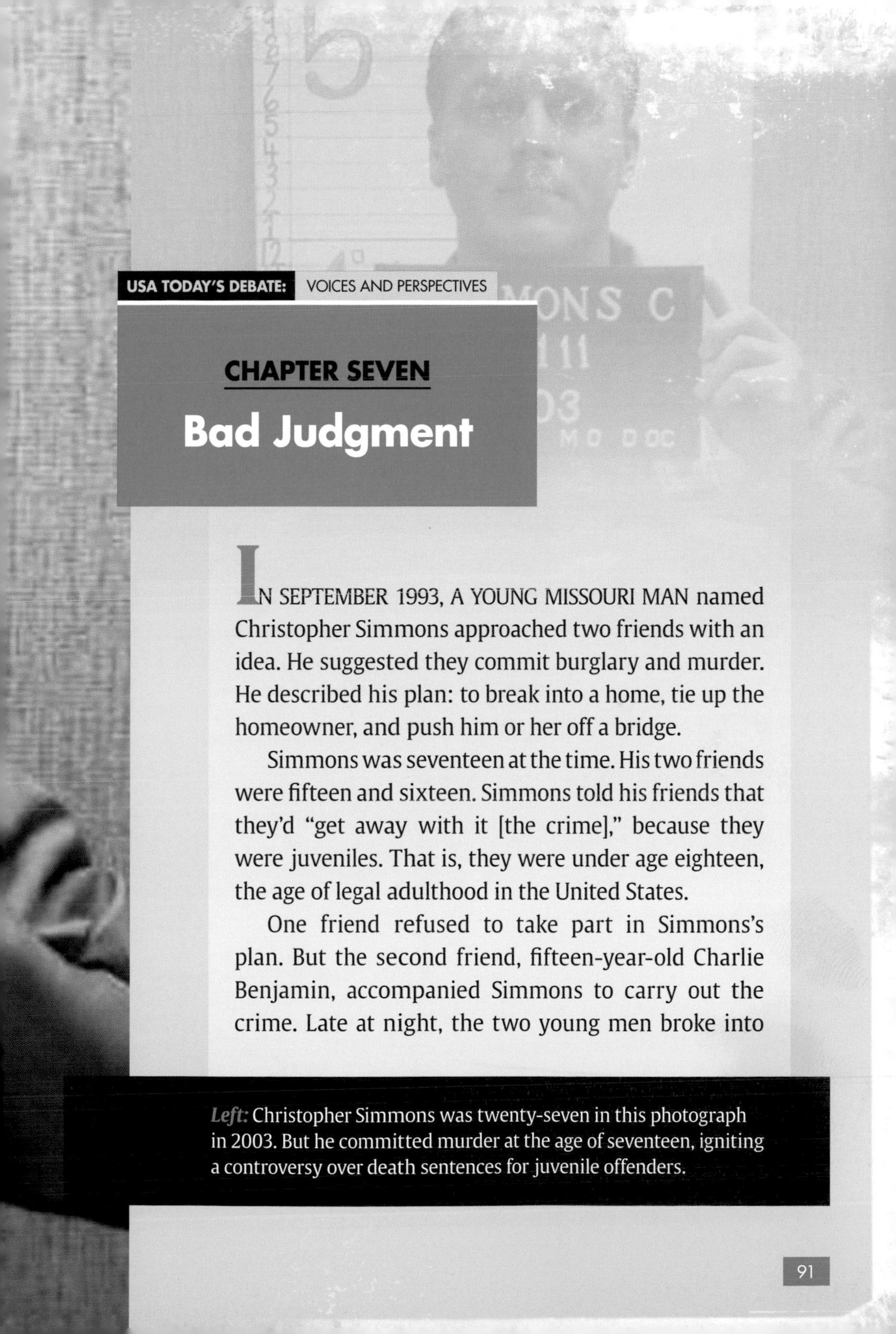

## CHAPTER SEVEN

# Bad Judgment

IN SEPTEMBER 1993, A YOUNG MISSOURI MAN named Christopher Simmons approached two friends with an idea. He suggested they commit burglary and murder. He described his plan: to break into a home, tie up the homeowner, and push him or her off a bridge.

Simmons was seventeen at the time. His two friends were fifteen and sixteen. Simmons told his friends that they'd "get away with it [the crime]," because they were juveniles. That is, they were under age eighteen, the age of legal adulthood in the United States.

One friend refused to take part in Simmons's plan. But the second friend, fifteen-year-old Charlie Benjamin, accompanied Simmons to carry out the crime. Late at night, the two young men broke into

*Left:* Christopher Simmons was twenty-seven in this photograph in 2003. But he committed murder at the age of seventeen, igniting a controversy over death sentences for juvenile offenders.

the home of Shirley Crook. Crook awakened when she heard the intruders. Simmons and Benjamin ordered her out of bed, bound her hands behind her back with duct tape, and taped her eyes and mouth shut. They then drove her in her minivan to a nearby state park.

During the van ride, Crook was able to free her hands. So Simmons and Benjamin retied her, this time using electrical cable, leather straps, and cloth. They tied her hands and feet together, covered her face completely with duct tape, and pushed her off a railroad bridge into the Meramec River. Crook drowned in the river.

Simmons was arrested at high school the next day. The police handled him roughly, and he soon confessed to the crime. Simmons believed that his juvenile status would save him from harsh punishment, since prosecutors, juries, and judges frequently treat young offenders with compassion. But in 1993, the law allowed the death penalty for juveniles—and that's the

Shirley Crook's gruesome death in the Meramec River *(above)* in Missouri added to the debate over the death penalty sentence for her juvenile killer.

punishment prosecutors chose to pursue in the Simmons case.

In June 1994, a jury found Simmons guilty of capital murder. During the penalty phase of the trial, the jury heard testimony from Shirley Crook's family members. They spoke emotionally about their loss and the gruesome way Crook had died. They asked the jury to sentence Simmons to death for his crimes.

Simmons's defense attorneys didn't present a forceful argument. They called Simmons a good brother, a loving son, and a helpful friend, and they asked the jury to spare his life. But the jury chose death for Christopher Simmons.

Like most death penalty cases, the Simmons case then entered the appeals system. While living on Missouri's death row, Simmons got a new team of lawyers. They argued his case more aggressively than his original defense team. They told the court that Simmons was a troubled young man. He had suffered severe physical and mental abuse at the hands of his stepfather and had been addicted to drugs and alcohol at the time he had killed Shirley Crook. They argued that his troubled upbringing had led him to commit murder. He certainly deserved punishment, the lawyers argued, but not the ultimate punishment of execution. The appeals court rejected this argument and upheld the original death sentence.

Eventually, in 2003, the Simmons case reached the Missouri Supreme Court. By this time, Christopher Simmons had been on death row for nine years. During this time, he had become a model prisoner. He had devoted some of his time in prison to counseling other young people against crime and drug use.

Simmons was by then twenty-seven years old. He was no longer a juvenile. But the Missouri Supreme Court ruled in his case that executing people for crimes they had committed as juveniles amounted to cruel and unusual punishment, in violation of the Eighth Amendment of the U.S. Constitution. Thus it would be unconstitutional to execute Simmons for his crime. His sentence was changed to life in prison without parole.

The state of Missouri was unhappy with the ruling. It took the case to the U.S. Supreme Court, hoping to restore Simmons's death sentence. Once it reached the Supreme Court, the case—by then known as *Roper v. Simmons*—became a lightning rod for death penalty opponents and death penalty supporters.

## OLD ENOUGH TO KILL, OLD ENOUGH TO DIE?

In the United States, the law treats juveniles differently than adults. People under the age of eighteen are not allowed to vote, cannot join the military without a parent's permission, cannot serve on juries, cannot legally buy cigarettes or alcohol, and cannot enter into legal contracts. The government makes such laws in recognition of the fact that young people aren't always capable of making sound decisions.

Yet in 2004, when *Roper v. Simmons* arrived at the U.S. Supreme Court, the law did not distinguish between adults and juveniles in the matter of executions. Although they were too young to vote and buy cigarettes, seventeen-year-olds—and in some states sixteen-year-olds—were old enough to be put to death for their crimes. Since 1976 more than twenty people had been executed in the United States for crimes they had committed as juveniles.

> **"Easily influenced and unable to foresee the results of their actions, teenagers are denied the right to vote and buy alcohol. Why, then, do they earn the right to be executed?"**
>
> —WILLIAM SCHULZ, AMNESTY INTERNATIONAL
>
> USA TODAY · NOVEMBER 12, 2002 · Letter to the Editor

Death penalty opponents found this situation absurd. They argued that it was barbaric for the state to impose the death penalty on children. In 2004 the American Civil Liberties Union, a strong force in the movement to abolish the death penalty, noted that "internationally, the execution of juveniles is largely considered inhuman . . . and in direct conflict with fundamental principles of justice." The ACLU continued:

> Ironically, many of the countries that the United States government regularly criticizes for human rights abuses have abolished the practice of executing juveniles. For example, between 1994 and 2000, Yemen, Zimbabwe, China and parts of Pakistan amended their laws to prohibit the execution of juvenile offenders. In continuing what is universally viewed as a barbaric and uncivilized practice, the United States has, over the past decade, executed more juvenile offenders than every other nation in the world combined.

Death penalty opponents knew that *Roper v. Simmons* would be a watershed case, and they rallied to Simmons's support. They argued on his behalf that young people were less capable than adults of planning, exercising self-control, and making good decisions—and therefore should not be held to the same standards as adults when it came to crime and punishment. They said that Simmons's history of mental and physical abuse, as well as his drug and alcohol addiction, had clouded his judgment at the age of seventeen. They even presented scientific studies showing that the brains of young people were very different from the brains of adults.

Death penalty supporters also had strong feelings about the case. The victims' rights group Justice For All argued that Simmons, at the age of seventeen, had been plenty old enough to know right from wrong when he killed Shirley Crook. Simmons "specifically knew it was wrong to kill, understood the consequences of his actions, and nevertheless committed a horrific premeditated murder of an innocent woman," JFA argued.

October 12, 2004 · *Guest Editorial*

# U.S. should join the world in halting juvenile executions

From the Pages of USA TODAY

**The Forum**

Today, the U.S. Supreme Court will hear *Roper vs. Simmons*, a case about whether the execution of children constitutes cruel and unusual punishment under the U.S. Constitution.

Christopher Simmons was 17 when he and an accomplice murdered a woman while attempting to rob her.

Missouri's high court ruled that Simmons should not be executed because a national consensus has developed against the capital punishment of offenders younger than 18. Missouri appealed the ruling to the U.S. Supreme Court.

I am hopeful our top court will take this opportunity to acknowledge that evolving standards of decency at home and abroad—as well as basic principles of American justice—require the rejection of executing children once and for all.

Opposition to juvenile capital punishment has gained significant momentum in the past few years in the United States.

Federal law and the laws of 31 states now prohibit death sentences for individuals who committed crimes before their 18th birthdays. Just this year, South Dakota and Wyoming banned the juvenile death penalty. This national trend echoes an even more dramatic evolution of international consensus. Almost universally, the peoples and nations of the world have condemned the juvenile death penalty as inhumane.

In the past three years, the only nations known to have executed juveniles are China, Iran and the United States.

**Counters basic principles**

Citizens and lawmakers in every state have recognized that the juvenile death penalty is inconsistent with the principles of our justice system, which punishes offenders in proportion to their culpability [guilt].

Proponents of executing juveniles argue that adolescents are sufficiently responsible for their actions to justify imposing the same sentences as those given to adults.

Medical and scientific experts disagree. Cutting-edge research shows that the parts of the brain associated with impulse control, long-range planning, judgment and a full appreciation of consequences continue to mature throughout adolescence.

Americans have long understood this intuitively. We limit or prohibit teens from driving, smoking, drinking and voting because we know that their capacities for curbing impulsiveness, using sound judgment and exercising self-control are much less developed.

Though these facts in no way minimize the suffering of victims and victims' families, they should influence the sentences juvenile offenders receive.

**Global consensus**

The elimination of the juvenile death penalty would be a significant step in bringing the U.S. in line with the moral consensus of the global community. The Founders of our great nation celebrated the need for "a decent Respect to the Opinions of Mankind" in our Declaration of Independence. Since the end of World War II [1939–1945], our country has taken the lead in speaking out against human-rights violations elsewhere in the world and has enjoyed respect in world affairs.

The American system of constitutional democracy and guaranteed freedoms has stood as an exemplar [model] in the eyes of people and nations emerging from totalitarian and repressive regimes. The continued policy of executing juveniles detracts profoundly from our credibility as a champion of human rights and, therefore, erodes our ability to influence the behavior of other nations and world leaders.

While almost universal condemnation of the juvenile death penalty has become as well recognized as the global prohibitions against slavery, torture and genocide, in America we have executed more juveniles in the past 15 years than all other countries combined.

For all of these reasons, I joined a "friend of the court" brief [letter of support] to the Supreme Court in this case. Nobel Peace Prize winners, including former Russian president Mikhail Gorbachev, South African Archbishop Desmond Tutu and the Tibetan Dalai Lama all have encouraged the court to reject juvenile capital punishment. I fervently hope the jurists will agree with these esteemed peacemakers.

Our nation is now acknowledging what the rest of the world already knows: Executing juvenile offenders is cruel and inhumane.

—Former U.S. president Jimmy Carter

JFA also stressed that juveniles are each different when it comes to maturity, experience, intelligence, and morality. It said that the U.S. legal system should not group all juvenile offenders together as a class, with a specific cutoff age for execution, but instead should consider each case individually.

On March 1, 2005, the Supreme Court made its ruling. In a close five-to-four decision, it agreed with the lower court that executing juvenile murderers amounted to cruel and unusual punishment. The ruling was greeted with cheers from the anti–death penalty community, both nationally and worldwide.

The ruling had widespread implications for other juvenile murderers. At the time, seventy inmates were on death row for crimes committed as juveniles. The Court's ruling invalidated their death sentences.

## WINDOW ON THE BRAIN

During the Simmons case, anti–death penalty opponents cited scientific studies about the human brain. These studies, conducted at Harvard University Medical School, the National Institute of Mental Health, and the Department of Neuroscience at the University of California at Los Angeles (UCLA), suggested that the human brain is not fully developed until the age of eighteen to twenty-two. Specifically, the prefrontal cortex—the part of the brain that allows humans to plan, control their impulses, and anticipate the consequences of their actions—is last to develop. If these studies are accurate, they show that juveniles are more likely than adults to act impulsively and make bad decisions.

Death penalty opponents were quick to latch onto the brain studies. They used them to argue that Christopher Simmons and other juvenile murderers were not calculating, cold-blooded killers but instead were immature and impulsive criminals who did not deserve execution. But death penalty supporters denounced the brain studies. Dianne Clements, president of Justice For All, called the studies "junk science." "This is an effort

> **"[Christopher Simmons] was a young man who planned and carried out a horrible murder that took time and effort and a lot of thinking. Do you mean to tell me that for the whole time he was doing this, his brain wasn't working as an adult?"**
>
> —**DIANNE CLEMENTS,** JUSTICE FOR ALL, A PRO-DEATH PENALTY ORGANIZATION
>
> USA TODAY · OCTOBER 12, 2004

by those in the scientific community who oppose the death penalty to use science to argue their position," Clements said.

The brain studies remain controversial. They pose important questions about juveniles and the ability to know right from wrong. But what about people who are mentally ill? Do they know right from wrong? Should they be sentenced to death for a capital crime?

Over the years, U.S. courts have tried to address these questions. A 1986 Supreme Court decision, *Ford v. Wainwright*, prohibits the execution of an insane person. But in death penalty cases, the legal definition of insanity is strict. To be labeled insane, it must be clear that an inmate cannot understand the reason for or the reality of his or her punishment. Many people on death row suffer from lesser forms of mental illness that do not qualify them as "insane," so they are therefore eligible for execution. In a few cases, prison doctors have even treated mentally ill people with psychiatric medication to make them "sane enough" to face execution.

In 2002, in *Atkins v. Virginia*, the Supreme Court ruled that executing people with mental retardation amounted to cruel and unusual punishment. Some death penalty supporters, including Supreme Court justice Antonin Scalia (who voted against the decision), oppose *Atkins v. Virginia*. They argue that even mentally retarded people should know the difference between right and wrong. Death penalty supporters also charge that some inmates exaggerate their mental deficiencies as a ploy to get off death row.

Death penalty opponents argue that states have wrongly executed many mentally impaired people, including those who lacked the intelligence and sanity to understand their crimes and punishment. For example, one death row inmate wanted to put Jesus Christ and President John F. Kennedy (dead since 1963) on the witness stand during his trial. Another set aside the dessert from his last meal, believing he would be able to eat it later.

*Above:* Antonin Scalia is one of several justices on the U.S. Supreme Court who favor the death penalty.

### A TROUBLED MIND

Insanity and mental retardation are recognized forms of mental illness. Many people on death row are mentally troubled but have not been labeled insane or mentally retarded. In evaluating death row inmates, psychiatrists have found that most of them grew up in abusive homes. They frequently suffered beatings and sexual abuse as children. Many lived in extreme poverty. They responded to abuse, despair, and violence by becoming violent themselves.

In trying to keep a defendant off death row, defense attorneys often point out the defendant's troubled childhood as a way to explain criminal behavior. For example, Christopher Simmons's lawyers stressed Simmons's cruel abuse at the hands of his stepfather when trying to win his release from death row. Such an argument can make a defendant appear more human and vulnerable and might arouse sympathy among judges and juries.

Does a troubled childhood excuse criminal behavior? Death penalty supporters are quick to say no. "Over and over we are told by these anti–death penalty activists that a grim upbringing somehow excuses a vicious, brutal and senseless murder," writes one pro–death penalty website. "We never hear one word from them about the innocent victims of these killers; only that we should show sympathy and understanding for the murderer."

## CHAPTER EIGHT

# At Random?

IN 2001 GARY LEON RIDGWAY, KNOWN AS THE Green River Killer, confessed to the murder of forty-eight women in the Seattle/Tacoma area of Washington State. Ridgway had carried out the killings in the early 1980s. Most of his victims had been female prostitutes or teenage runaways. Ridgway strangled them, usually dumping their bodies in or near the Green River outside Seattle.

It might be assumed that in a state with the death penalty, such as Washington, the confessed and convicted killer of forty-eight people would automatically receive the death penalty for his crimes. But Gary Ridgway did not get the death penalty. He made a deal with prosecutors.

*Left:* Gary Ridgway received a sentence of life in prison without the possibility of parole for the murders of forty-eight people in Washington State in the early 1980s.

They agreed to spare his life if he would help them identify and locate the remains of his victims. Prosecutors hesitated to make the deal. They knew it would be unpopular with the public and victims' families. But without Ridgway's cooperation, prosecutors would have been able to conclude only seven of the Green River murder cases. With Ridgway's help, they were able to identify forty-one additional victims.

Gary Ridgway is serving forty-eight life sentences, with no possibility of parole. Meanwhile, all across the country, killers who took one life are on death row, awaiting execution. Is that fair? How is it that some killers get the death penalty while others get LWOP for more severe crimes? The answer exposes some of the inconsistencies in the U.S. death penalty system.

## WHO DECIDES?

In *Furman v. Georgia*, the Supreme Court halted executions because they were being carried out in random and arbitrary ways. Death penalty opponents say that nothing has changed since that ruling in 1972. They say death sentences are still handed out randomly.

In truth, no hard and fast rules govern the decision of whether or not to pursue the death penalty after a capital crime. The decision is left to the local district attorney (DA). In Tyler, Texas, DAs decided to pursue the death penalty for John Luttig's killer but not for Ivan Holland's killers. Philadelphia DA Lynne Abraham seeks the death penalty for 80 percent of all eligible murders in her district. At the same time, other DAs rarely or never pursue the death penalty.

Why not always pursue the death penalty for capital crimes? For one thing, death penalty cases cost more money than non–death penalty cases. The law requires two trials in death penalty cases—one for conviction and another for sentencing. Then there is the lengthy appeals process, which can cost taxpayers hundreds of thousands—or even millions—of dollars. District attorneys may have more cases that qualify

## The U.S. Constitution and the Evolving Standard of Decency

The death penalty debate frequently centers on the U.S. Constitution, specifically the Eighth Amendment, which forbids cruel and unusual punishment. Clearly, Americans who wrote the Constitution didn't think execution was cruel and unusual. Execution was widespread in the early United States, and the Fifth Amendment, which guarantees people's rights in criminal cases, specifically mentions capital crimes.

But in modern times, the Supreme Court has declared the death penalty to be cruel and unusual under certain circumstances. How is it that a punishment that was once considered perfectly reasonable later became "cruel and unusual"? The Court explains the situation by describing an "evolving standard of decency" in the United States. This is a legalistic way of saying that ideas about cruelty change as U.S. society matures. So while execution was not considered cruel or unusual when the Constitution was written in 1787, in our modern and more advanced society, it is seen as cruel and unusual in certain instances.

for the death penalty than governments have money to pay for them. And because local governments have limited budgets, district attorneys must pick and choose which death penalty cases to pursue.

After a murder, especially a high-profile case like the John Luttig killing, citizens often feel outraged. They often pressure police, prosecutors, and judges to arrest and punish the killer. They push prosecutors to seek the death penalty—especially when the victim is a "valued citizen," such as a police officer, a prominent businessperson, or a public official. But citizens are less likely to clamor for the death penalty when the victim is a prostitute, a drug addict, or a homeless person. That's because society unfairly views some people as more valuable than others. And this bias spills over into the death penalty system.

## PLAYING POLITICS

Attitudes toward crime and punishment have changed over more than two centuries of U.S. history. In earlier eras, many people were interested in rehabilitating or reforming criminals—that is, helping them become better citizens. In the twenty-first century, however, many citizens want politicians and law enforcement officials to get "tough on crime." They are less interested in rehabilitating criminals than in locking them up—and executing them in some cases. In some places, if a prosecutor wants to become a judge (an elected or appointed position, depending on the state) or run for the state legislature, it helps to have a "tough on crime" record, including a record of winning death penalty cases.

Judges also want to appear tough on crime. Penny White, an elected judge on Tennessee's state supreme court, learned the hard way that many U.S. voters want hard-nosed judges when it comes to capital punishment.

> **"We used to want to rehabilitate [reform] the offender. Now it's all vengeance and deterrence—even though there's no convincing evidence the death penalty is a deterrent."**
>
> —JUDGE GILBERT MERRITT, FEDERAL APPEALS COURT, 1992

After White took a stand against the death penalty in the early 1990s, her political opponents accused her of "favoring the rights of criminals over the rights of victims." She was not reelected to the court.

Historically, the Democratic Party has opposed the death penalty, and the Republican Party supports it. But that's not always the case. President Bill Clinton, a Democrat, favored the death penalty and signed several tough death penalty laws during his two terms in office (1992–2000). When Texas governor George W. Bush ran for president in 2000, he highlighted his state's aggressive pursuit of capital punishment. During Bush's term as governor, Texas had executed an average of one person every two weeks. Partly because of his law-and-order attitude, Bush was a favorite with many voters.

> **"Nothing becomes politics quite like death. With a presidential election approaching [in 2008] and three important cases before the Supreme Court, the country is once again grappling with the death penalty. Politicians and citizens alike are debating how—and whether—we should kill those who kill others."**
>
> —PROFESSOR JONATHAN TURLEY,
> GEORGE WASHINGTON UNIVERSITY LAW SCHOOL, WASHINGTON, D.C.
> USA TODAY · JANUARY 16, 2008 · Editorial

### "THE DEATH BELT"

If you kill someone in Michigan, you will definitely not get the death penalty because Michigan has no death penalty. If you kill someone in New Hampshire, a death penalty state, you still probably won't get the death penalty. New Hampshire has never sentenced anyone to death since the death penalty was reinstated there in 1991. But if you kill someone in Texas, assuming you're convicted and the murder is a capital crime, your chances of getting the death penalty are strong. Texas has carried out about 37 percent of all executions in the United States since 1977. Eleven percent of U.S. death row inmates are in Texas.

Bill Moffitt, past president of the National Association of Criminal Defense Lawyers, explains the high numbers in Texas this way: "To begin with, Texas has a certain Wild West mentality. You combine that with politicians pandering to their constituents [voters], who greatly favor capital punishment, and you come up with the current situation."

Texas is called the "buckle on the Death Belt"—the "Death Belt" being a group of states that carry out the most executions in the nation. Texas tops the list with 435 executions since 1977. Next comes Virginia (103), Oklahoma (89), Florida (67), Missouri (66), Georgia (44), North Carolina (43), South Carolina (41), Alabama (40), Arkansas (27), and Louisiana (27). With the exception of Missouri, all these states are in the South. Polls show that southerners favor the death penalty more than people in other parts of the country. In addition, the South has the nation's highest murder rate, which may explain the increased support for capital punishment there.

People who oppose the death penalty often cite its randomness—the fact that it is applied in some cases and not others—as a reason for their opposition. Death penalty supporters do not deny that the U.S. death penalty system is a patchwork of different laws and practices, varying by state and municipality. They are less concerned by the randomness of executions in the United States and more committed to seeing that where the death penalty is legal and applicable, it is carried out fairly and efficiently, and with respect for victims' rights.

USA TODAY

**News**

SECTION A

**February 4, 1998**

# Texas Executes Tucker

From the Pages of USA TODAY

HUNTSVILLE, Texas—Pickax killer and born-again Christian Karla Faye Tucker was executed at a Texas prison Tuesday after she and an unusual coalition of supporters lost a widely publicized fight to save her life.

Tucker, 38, was pronounced dead at 6:45 p.m. CST [central standard time], eight minutes after lethal drugs began flowing into her outstretched arms. She is the first woman executed in Texas since the Civil War.

When asked if she had final words, Tucker turned to the families of her victims and said, "I am so sorry. I hope God will give you peace with this.

"I am going to be face to face with Jesus now," Tucker said to her family. "I love all of you very much. I will see you all when you get there."

When she finished her statement, Tucker licked her lips and appeared to pray. Witness Michael Graczyk of the Associated Press, said that as the drugs began taking effect Tucker gasped slightly twice, then let out a five-to-10-second wheeze as the air escaped her lungs. Her eyes remained nearly wide open and her mouth was slightly open.

Tucker and companion Daniel Garrett were convicted of killing Jerry Lynn Dean, 27, and Deborah Thornton, 32, on June 13, 1983, at Dean's Houston [Texas] apartment. Richard Thornton, Deborah Thornton's husband, witnessed the execution. "The world's a better place," Thornton said after Tucker died.

The execution came less than an hour after Tucker's final appeals were turned down by the U.S. Supreme Court and Gov. George W. Bush announced he would not grant a 30-day reprieve.

"May God bless Karla Faye Tucker, and God bless her victims and their families," Bush said. Eleventh-hour appeals also were rejected by a state court and the 5th U.S. Circuit Court of Appeals in New Orleans.

Tucker's case became known worldwide after pleas for mercy from Pope John Paul II, Christian Coalition founder Pat Robertson and the Rev. Jesse Jackson.

The last woman executed in the U.S. was Velma Barfield, also a born-again Christian, in 1984. She died in North Carolina for lacing her boyfriend's food with rat poison.

—Peter Katel

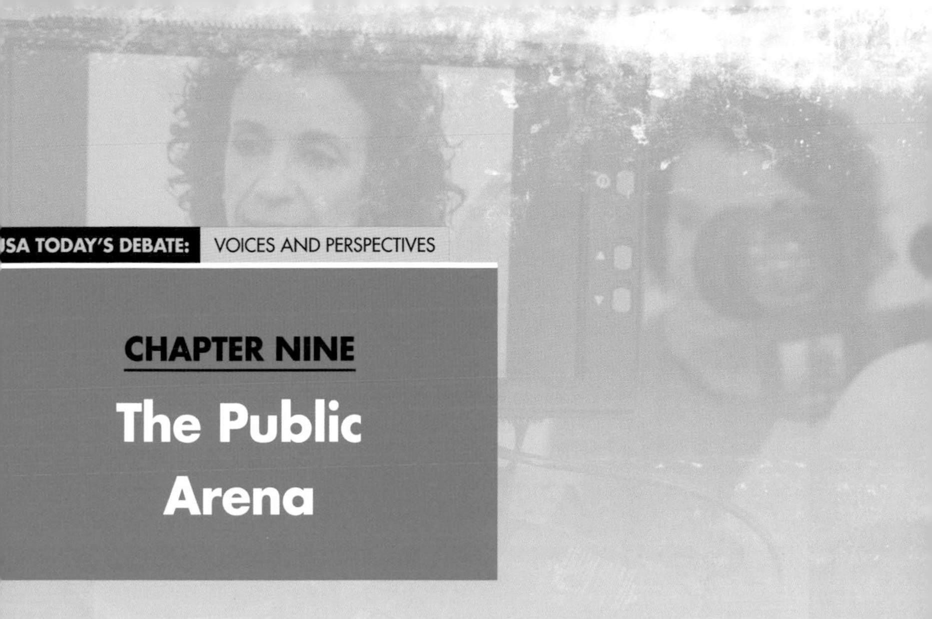

## CHAPTER NINE

# The Public Arena

THE JUSTICE FOR ALL WEBSITE OFFERS A VARIETY of information on legislation, resources, and news of interest to crime victims and their families. On the "death penalty" link, the website gives the following statement:

> If you search the internet via search engines for "death penalty," you are likely to find thousands, if not tens of thousands of "hits" to web sites related to the topic. With very few exceptions, these sites are anti-death penalty. Is this because the majority of people are against the death penalty? Not according to recent surveys. It is simply because people who are adamantly opposed to the death penalty tend to

*Left:* Lisa Green, a deputy district attorney in Bakersfield, California, speaks to the media after a death sentence trial in 2008.

> take an activist stance and become involved in working to stop the death penalty. For the most part, people who support the death penalty do so quietly, in their own minds and feel no need to do so in any public fashion. It is the law and they expect it to be carried out.

This statement accurately sums up the situation regarding the death penalty and U.S. public opinion. Thousands of websites,

***Above, from left:*** Delroy Lindo, Aidan Quinn, and Stockard Channing starred in *The Exonerated*, a 2002 play based on the real cases of death row inmates who were released from death row.

organizations, movies, plays, articles, books, and studies spell out the flaws, inconsistencies, and injustices of the death penalty. Yet most Americans still support it. What's going on?

The Gallup organization conducts regular polls of U.S. opinion regarding the death penalty. In 2007 a poll revealed that 69 percent of Americans favored the death penalty for murderers. Pollsters also found that 49 percent of Americans felt that the death penalty wasn't imposed often enough.

In a 2003 poll, Gallup asked Americans why they supported the death penalty. More than half talked about justice, fairness, and revenge. They cited the biblical saying "an eye for an eye" and said the punishment should fit the crime. Other respondents thought the death penalty would save taxpayers money (11 percent) or that it would deter future crime (11 percent). A few gave other reasons for their support, such as the belief that the death penalty helped bring a feeling of closure, relief, or justice to victims' families.

## DIGGING DEEPER

In 2004 Gallup compiled information on death penalty views and demographics, such as party affiliation, gender, and race. Here's how the numbers broke down:

| | **Favor Death Penalty** | **Oppose Death Penalty** | **No Opinion** |
|---|---|---|---|
| Republicans | 80% | 17% | 3% |
| Independents | 65% | 30% | 5% |
| Democrats | 58% | 36% | 6% |
| Men | 74% | 23% | 3% |
| Women | 62% | 32% | 6% |
| Whites | 71% | 24% | 5% |
| Blacks | 44% | 49% | 7% |

USA TODAY
News
SECTION A

December 14, 2005

# Williams executed, but controversy remains

From the Pages of USA TODAY

SAN FRANCISCO—The execution of gangster Stanley "Tookie" Williams is one more dramatic push moving the nation closer to abolishing the death penalty. Or it is the criminal justice system duly working to rid society of a brutal and remorseless killer.

That was the contradictory spin—absent any apparent national fallout—in the aftermath of the Crips street gang co-founder's death by lethal injection early Tuesday in one of the most publicized capital punishment cases in years.

Death penalty opponents such as Jesse Jackson, actor Mike Farrell and 2,000 others who demonstrated outside San Quentin State Prison during Williams' final hours saw a troubling disregard for his claims of innocence and rehabilitation. Supporters, including relatives of his victims, were troubled only that it took nearly a quarter-century to execute a man convicted of murdering four people with a shotgun.

The Williams case underscores an enduring public divide over the death penalty. Nearly two-thirds of Americans support executions, but Gallup Polls since 2000 have found that as many as 40% believe capital punishment is applied unfairly in the USA.

Advances in DNA testing that have freed some death row inmates and slowed the pace of executions put heightened scrutiny on the death penalty. While the Supreme Court endorses capital punishment, the justices have shown a growing desire to make sure accused killers get due process [fair trials] and able lawyers.

Moreover, the system discriminates, minority groups charge. Blacks make up 12% of the population, but 42% of the condemned, the NAACP says. In the 38 death penalty states, 98% of prosecutors are white, only 2% black or Latino, it says.

The 51-year-old bodybuilder had exhausted his appeals and been denied clemency by Gov. Arnold Schwarzenegger. Led shackled and handcuffed into the death chamber at midnight, he declined to give a formal statement. He seemed frustrated, according to an Associated Press reporter who watched the execution, as officials struggled to insert intravenous lines into his muscular arms.

About 15 minutes later, he appeared to ask one of the men working with the needle, "You doing that right?" the AP [Associated Press] said. He appeared to stop breathing just moments after a prison official read the death warrant.

Schwarzenegger, who had denied two clemency bids for two other condemned men, said he spent many hours reviewing the record in Williams' case before concluding that mercy wasn't justified. Politically, his decision buoyed flagging support among his Republican base, particularly conservatives, says Jack Pitney, a government professor at Claremont McKenna College outside Los Angeles. Clemency would have appealed mostly to liberals unlikely to vote for his re-election next year.

A 2001 Field Poll found 73% of Californians favoring a moratorium on executions while the death penalty's reliability is studied. The Death Penalty Information Center, which opposes capital punishment, estimates that 122 condemned inmates across the country have been freed from death rows since 1973 after proving their innocence.

Williams, too, claimed innocence and insisted that he couldn't express remorse for murders he never committed. Lack of remorse was a factor that Schwarzenegger said influenced his decision not to spare Williams.

—John Ritter

In 2003 Gallup asked people who opposed the death penalty to list reasons for their opposition. The numbers broke down as follows (some people gave more than one answer):

| | |
|---|---|
| It's wrong to take a life | 46% |
| People might be wrongly convicted | 25% |
| Punishment should be left to God | 13% |
| Murderers need to suffer and think about their crimes in prison | 5% |
| Murderers could possibly be rehabilitated [reformed] | 5% |
| It depends on the circumstances | 4% |
| The death penalty is applied unfairly | 4% |
| The death penalty is not a deterrent for future murderers | 4% |
| Other | 3% |
| No opinion | 4% |

These numbers give a snapshot of U.S. public opinion about the death penalty in the early years of the twenty-first century. The statistics show that Republicans, men, and whites are more likely to support the death penalty than Democrats, women, and African Americans and that those who oppose the death penalty tend to do so for ethical reasons.

But poll numbers change constantly. Experts explain that the changing numbers reflect the mood of the American public at any given moment. For instance, in 1966 support for capital punishment reached its all-time low. At that time, many people were concerned about civil rights, social justice, and racial equality. They thought the death penalty was being applied unfairly. Support for the death penalty rose steadily through the 1970s and 1980s, possibly because murder rates were rising in these same decades. In 1994 support for capital punishment reached its all-time high—80 percent. People were worried about murder and other violent crime. They wanted lawmakers to get tough with criminals.

In the first decade of the 2000s, support for capital punishment has gone up and down. In 2001, 67 percent of Americans favored capital punishment. In 2002 the number rose to 71 percent. Social scientists think that the 9/11 terrorist attacks in late 2001 might have contributed to this increase. In 2008 support for the death penalty was lower, with 64 percent of Americans favoring its use. Experts think that the increased use of DNA testing to prove prisoners' innocence might have led some people to withdraw their support for the death penalty.

**PRO/CON**

As the Justice For All website explains, the anti–death penalty movement seems to be much more vocal and organized than the pro–death penalty movement. Hundreds of groups are working to temporarily halt and eventually abolish the death penalty in the United States. These groups include the National Coalition to Abolish the Death Penalty, the ACLU, the NAACP, the Moratorium Campaign, Amnesty International USA, the Campaign to End the Death Penalty, and many more.

The groups use a variety of tools to advance their cause. They send letters and petitions to local, state, and federal lawmakers; conduct studies about the death penalty; take part in death penalty trials and appeals; counsel and assist death penalty defendants and inmates; write letters to death row inmates; hold protests

> **"The death penalty represents the pointless and needless extinction of life with only marginal contributions to any discernable [obvious] social or public purpose."**
>
> —**JUSTICE JOHN PAUL STEVENS,** U.S. SUPREME COURT
>
> **USA TODAY · APRIL 17, 2008**

at execution sites; and produce educational materials such as books and websites. The groups raise money through membership dues, donations from individuals and businesses, grants from foundations, and fund-raisers such as concerts and auctions.

Pro-death penalty forces are less visible, but they are by no means weak or disorganized. After all, a majority of Americans support the death penalty, and it is the law of the land in thirty-five of the fifty U.S. states (70 percent). Pro-death penalty Americans show their support by voting for politicians who also support the death penalty. They also contact governors and other state officials, urging them not to overturn or delay death sentences. They conduct studies, produce websites, and write books and articles designed to advance the pro-death penalty argument. They sometimes gather outside execution sites, just as death penalty opponents, do—only the pro-death penalty forces attend to cheer the executions and to support victims' families.

The Republican Party, which dominated national politics in the early 2000s, supports the death penalty as part of its party platform. On the state and local

> **"Courts must have the option of imposing the death penalty in capital murder cases and other instances of heinous crime, while federal review of those sentences should be streamlined to focus on claims of innocence and to prevent delaying tactics by defense attorneys."**
>
> —**REPUBLICAN PARTY PLATFORM,** 2008

levels, many prosecutors, police officers, judges, state legislators, and other officials strongly support the death penalty. Victims' rights groups are usually pro–death penalty. Conservative groups—those that back traditional values such as law and order, religious devotion, and male-headed households—also tend to back the death penalty. Such groups include the National Rifle Association and Focus on the Family. Conservative columnists and radio talk show hosts frequently present pro–death penalty arguments to large audiences.

**CASE STUDY**

To learn more about pro- and anti–death penalty forces at work, consider the state of Minnesota. The state's last execution took place in 1906. The death penalty was abolished there in 1911. In 2003 the Minnesota governor, Republican Tim Pawlenty,

*Above:* Minnesota governor Tim Pawlenty speaks at the Republican National Convention in Saint Paul, Minnesota, in 2008. In 2003 Pawlenty led an effort to reinstate the death penalty in Minnesota.

## U.S. States and Jurisdictions without the Death Penalty

| | | |
|---|---|---|
| Alaska | Michigan | North Dakota |
| District of Columbia | Minnesota | Rhode Island |
| Hawaii | New Jersey | Vermont |
| Iowa | New Mexico | West Virginia |
| Maine | New York | Wisconsin |
| Massachusetts | | |

announced that he favored reinstatement of the death penalty in his state. Pawlenty told reporters he was fed up with crime in Minnesota. He wanted the worst murderers to pay the ultimate price for their actions. The governor's idea, backed by Republican state lawmakers, was to allow citizens to vote on a constitutional amendment that would reinstate the death penalty in Minnesota.

Once Pawlenty formulated his proposal, pro- and anti–death penalty forces went into action. Those opposed to the governor's idea formed Minnesotans Against the Death Penalty. The group immediately contacted state legislators, produced educational materials, raised funds, and organized citizens to fight the death penalty vote. Other anti–death penalty groups included Minnesota Advocates for Human Rights and the Minneapolis/Saint Paul chapter of Amnesty International. Pro–death penalty advocates included the governor, Republican state lawmakers, Republican voters, and many victims' families.

The fight played out through newspaper articles, radio shows, public meetings, educational forums, legislative hearings, press conferences, and committee meetings of the state legislature. During the debate, anti–death penalty voices talked about well-known problems with the death penalty: racism, poor legal representation, the chances of an innocent person being put to death, and the high costs of appeals. Pro–death penalty forces also expressed well-known arguments in favor of capital punishment: "an eye for an eye," justice for victims' families, the fear that murderers would be released to kill again, and deterrence.

In the end, Minnesotans never got to vote on whether or not to reinstate the death penalty. In May 2004, the state legislature rejected the bill that would have put the issue before voters, thus maintaining Minnesota's status as a non–death penalty state.

## FAITH AND THE DEATH PENALTY

Sometimes, it's easy to figure out where people stand on capital punishment, based on certain demographics. For example, conservatives and Republicans tend to support it strongly. Support is weaker among Democrats, African Americans, and liberals (people who support protection of political and civil liberties). People who belong to social justice and human rights organizations, such as Amnesty International, the NAACP, and the ACLU, are usually fiercely anti–death penalty.

When it comes to the connection between religious faith and positions on the death penalty, viewpoints are more difficult to categorize. For example, the Catholic Church officially opposes capital punishment, but more than half of U.S. Catholics support capital punishment. Protestants are also divided on the issue. Some Protestants cite passages from the Old Testament ("an eye for an eye") to back their arguments in favor of capital punishment. Other Protestants quote the New Testament ("turn the other cheek" and "love your enemies") to argue against the death penalty. Religious groups such as the Amish, Quakers, and Unitarians have a long tradition of pacifism (an antiwar philosophy) and are opposed to the death penalty. Many conservative Jews support capital punishment, while liberal Jews tend to oppose it. Muslims generally support the death penalty, a position put forth by the Quran, the holy book of Islam.

Pat Robertson, a prominent leader among Christian conservatives, surprised many when he spoke out about the death penalty in 1998. Robertson founded the Christian Coalition, one of the nation's foremost conservative political organizations and one that has long supported capital punishment. But when Karla Faye Tucker, a born-again Christian, faced execution in 1998, Robertson had a change

*Above:* Christian conservative Pat Robertson surprised many people when he spoke out against the death penalty in the late 1990s.

of heart. He argued that Tucker was a different person than the one who had committed murder in 1983. He said that executing her was "an act of barbarity that was totally unnecessary." Then Robertson went on to attack the death penalty in general. He denounced it as a brutal act of vengeance. He said it discriminated against minorities and the poor. He talked about mercy, clemency, and the need to protect life. Many members of the Christian Coalition were stunned by his turnaround. Death penalty opponents cheered Robertson's words.

Robertson's story is further proof that when it comes to the death penalty, it is hard to pin people down into categories. Religion, race, gender, and political party affiliation—none of these absolutely determines where a person might stand on the issue. In the end, the decision to support or oppose capital punishment is a highly personal one.

say

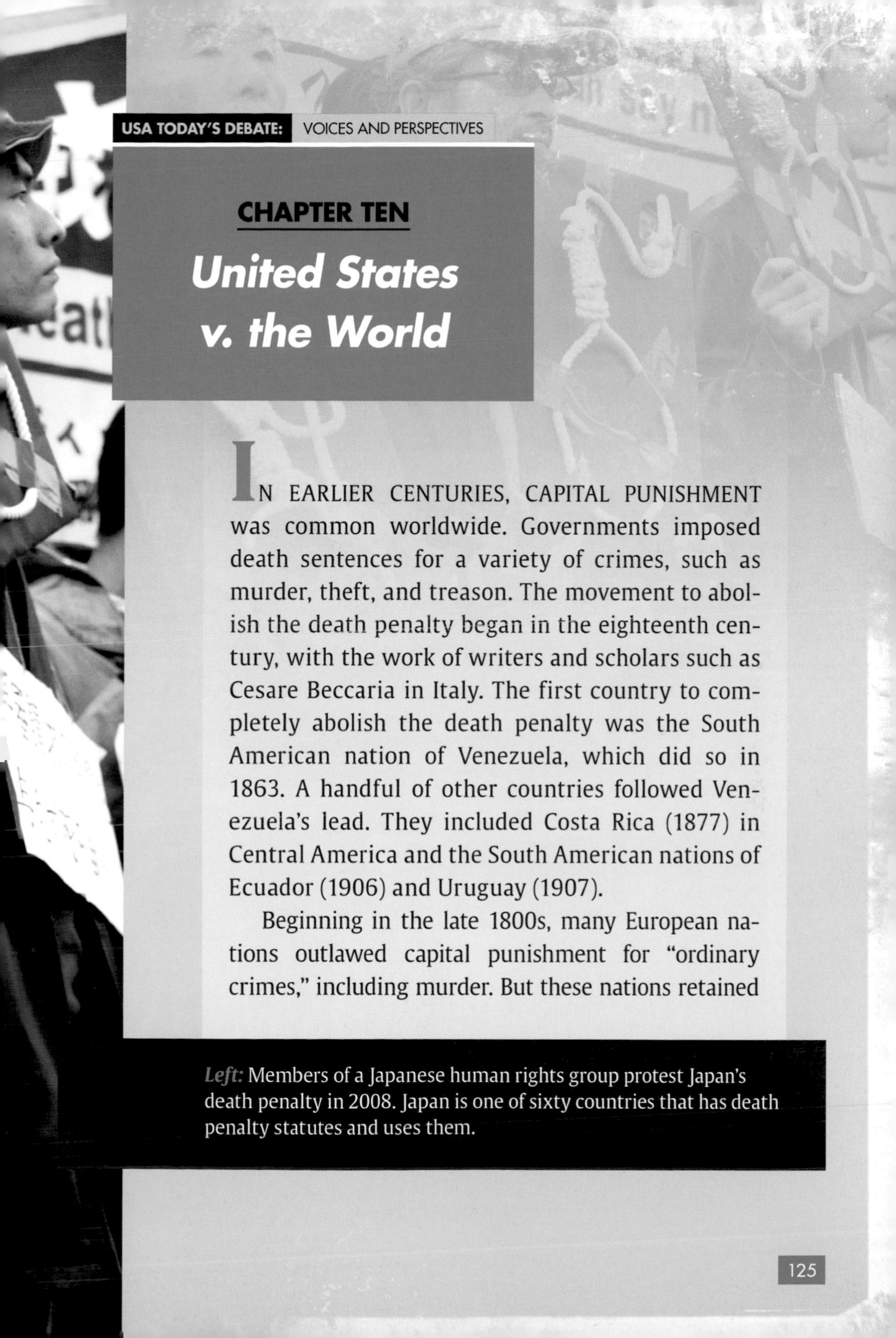

## CHAPTER TEN

# *United States v. the World*

IN EARLIER CENTURIES, CAPITAL PUNISHMENT was common worldwide. Governments imposed death sentences for a variety of crimes, such as murder, theft, and treason. The movement to abolish the death penalty began in the eighteenth century, with the work of writers and scholars such as Cesare Beccaria in Italy. The first country to completely abolish the death penalty was the South American nation of Venezuela, which did so in 1863. A handful of other countries followed Venezuela's lead. They included Costa Rica (1877) in Central America and the South American nations of Ecuador (1906) and Uruguay (1907).

Beginning in the late 1800s, many European nations outlawed capital punishment for "ordinary crimes," including murder. But these nations retained

*Left:* Members of a Japanese human rights group protest Japan's death penalty in 2008. Japan is one of sixty countries that has death penalty statutes and uses them.

capital punishment for "exceptional crimes," such as war crimes and genocide (the systematic killing of a racial, political, or cultural group). In 1867 Portugal was the first nation to abolish capital punishment for ordinary crimes. Then came the Netherlands (1870), Norway (1905), Sweden (1921), Denmark (1933), Switzerland (1942), Italy (1947), Finland (1949), and Austria (1950). Eventually, all these European nations abolished capital punishment completely.

World War II (1939–1945) had a significant impact on social attitudes in Europe, including attitudes toward capital punishment. During the war, the German government, led by

*Above:* Philippine president Gloria Macapagal-Arroyo *(left)* presents Pope Benedict XVI with a document abolishing the death penalty in the Philippines in 2006.

dictator Adolf Hitler, executed millions of Jews and other minority peoples across Europe. Shame and outrage at the killings led many Europeans to take a stand against state-sponsored executions. The abolitionist movement picked up speed in the following decades. Between 1976 and 2008, more than sixty countries around the world abolished the death penalty for all crimes. The most recent nation to do so was Uzbekistan in central Asia in 2008.

As of 2008, 91 of the world's 194 nations have no death penalty at all. Eleven nations reserve the death penalty for exceptional crimes but not ordinary crimes. Thirty-five countries have death penalty laws but have not carried out any executions in more than ten years.

More than half of the world's abolitionist countries are in Europe. That continent is the center of the international anti–death penalty movement. To join the European Union (a political and economic alliance of European nations), a country must first outlaw capital punishment. As part of its (so far unsuccessful) effort to win acceptance to the European Union, Turkey outlawed capital punishment in 2004.

Sixty countries (including the United States) have death penalty laws—and use them. According to Amnesty

**"My vote, when joined with at least four others, is in most cases the last step that permits an execution to proceed. I could not take part in that process if I believed what was being done to be immoral."**

**—ANTONIN SCALIA,**
U.S. SUPREME COURT JUSTICE, 2002

International, fifty-one nations sentenced at least 3,347 people to death in 2007. In that same year, twenty-four nations carried out at least 1,252 executions. Eighty-eight percent of these executions took place in just five countries: China, Iran, Pakistan, Saudi Arabia, and the United States. The number of people awaiting execution worldwide is unknown, but some researchers put the figure between about 18,000 and 27,500.

## THE COMPANY WE KEEP

Of all the criticism of the death penalty in the United States, some of the loudest voices come from the international community. The United Nations (UN;

*Above:* French president Jacques Chirac calls for universal abolition of the death penalty in front of the UN Commission on Human Rights in 2001.

an international peacekeeping and human rights organization) opposes the death penalty, as does the European Union. In 2004 the UN Commission on Human Rights issued a resolution calling on nations "to abolish the death penalty completely and, in the meantime, to establish a moratorium on executions."

Afghanistan, Iran, North Korea, Pakistan, Somalia, and Yemen—nations that are known for lawlessness, religious extremism, links to terrorism, and human rights violations, as well as for brutal methods of execution, such as beheading and stoning. Death penalty opponents say that as a developed, advanced nation, the United States should

> **"You are well aware of the European Union's determined stand on the abolition of the death penalty. It is based on the conviction that this penalty is contrary to human dignity."**
>
> —FRENCH PRESIDENT JACQUES CHIRAC,
> WRITING TO U.S. PRESIDENT BILL CLINTON, 2000
>
> USA TODAY · DECEMBER 14, 2000

Groups such as Amnesty International view the United States as barbaric and uncivilized in its use of the death penalty. These groups note that the United States is one of only a few industrialized, democratic nations that still execute citizens. And they point out that in using capital punishment, the United States keeps company with

join other developed nations in outlawing the death penalty.

Europeans are especially critical of capital punishment in the United States. In a few cases, European nations have refused to extradite, or hand over, U.S. criminals to U.S. authorities, because the criminals would have to face the death penalty back in the United States.

USA TODAY
News
SECTION A
November 2, 2006

# Court's role could reduce China's executions; Policy known as "kill fewer, kill carefully"

From the Pages of USA TODAY

BEIJING—China's move to give a top court final say on all death sentences should slow the furious pace of executions here, even though many non-violent offenses remain capital crimes, legal experts say.

Chinese legal scholars and lawyers welcomed this week's announcement by the government that the country's Supreme People's Court will review all capital punishment cases.

The change is "an important procedural step to prevent wrongful convictions," said China's top judge, Xiao Yang, according to the state-run Xinhua news service.

China was responsible for 81% of the world's known executions—1,770 out of 2,184—last year, according to Amnesty International. Amnesty said the actual number of executions in China could be several times higher. In the USA, 60 people were executed in 2005.

The reviews by the high court "should reduce the total number of executions by one-quarter or even a third," says Chen Weidong, a criminal law expert at People's University in Beijing.

Human rights groups and Chinese legal scholars have criticized the Chinese government for excessive use of the death penalty and for carrying out some executions after sham trials. Sixty-eight offenses—including non-violent crimes such as tax evasion, drug smuggling and corruption—carry the death penalty.

"The number of economic crimes that can be punished by the death penalty should gradually be cut," Chen says. "But it's hard to say if this will happen" in 2007 or later.

Recently, state media have exposed dozens of cases in which innocent people were sent to their deaths, including many who confessed after police beatings.

In response to the criticism, the government has introduced a series of reforms as part of a policy it calls "kill fewer, kill carefully."

In July, the government ordered that all death penalty appeals must be held in open court.

"We hope it leads to better-quality trials, but it's not automatic," says Mark Allison, who tracks death penalty cases for Amnesty International in Hong Kong. And although the government is likely to cut the number of executions by adding mandatory high court oversight, "execution numbers are still regarded as a state secret, so it will be impossible to measure," he said.

A growing lobby of Chinese lawyers and legal scholars has pushed for changes to current rules. Many lawyers charge minimal fees to represent those convicted of capital crimes in their appeals.

"The voices against the death penalty are growing louder," says Xuan Dong, a former judge who sent nearly 1,000 people to be executed in 25 years on the bench.

Xuan, now a defense lawyer and reform advocate at the Beijing firm King & Capital Lawyers, says he served the country by punishing crime, but "some defendants should not have been given the death penalty."

He Weifang, a professor at Beijing University's law school, says capital punishment is popular with a public weary of crime. "A huge portion [of Chinese] would reject abolishing the death penalty," he says.

Death penalty opponents, though, are urging Chinese filmmakers, writers and other artists to examine the subject in their work in hopes of broadening opposition.

Novels and movies could spur debate, much like the 1995 Hollywood film *Dead Man Walking*, he says. In the film, Susan Sarandon plays a Catholic nun who counsels a death row convict played by Sean Penn. The professor also wants Chinese courts to put all death sentence verdicts online within hours.

"If judicial decisions were open, we would know exactly how many were executed," he says, "and judges would be forced to be more conscientious."

—Calum MacLeod

American death row activists such as Mumia Abu-Jamal are heroes to some Europeans. But Europeans are not unified in their opposition to the death penalty. A 2005 Gallup poll showed that 55 percent of British citizens favor the death penalty for murderers. Polls of French and Italians reveal similar support for the death penalty. But most European leaders remain staunchly opposed to capital punishment.

### MIND YOUR OWN BUSINESS!

In the United States, death penalty supporters resent the criticism from Europe. After all, they say, the United States and Europe have very different cultural values. For one thing, the United States is much more violent than the nations of Europe. Americans have easy access to handguns, whereas European nations have strict gun-control laws. In 2002 the U.S. murder rate was 5.62 murders for every 100,000 inhabitants. The rate in Belgium that year was 1.5 murders per 100,000 inhabitants. Other murder rates (per 100,000 people) were 1.04 for Denmark, 1.11 for Germany, 1.12 for Italy, 2.92 for Switzerland, and 2.03 for the United Kingdom.

## International Methods of Execution

Beheading (Saudi Arabia, Iraq)
Electrocution (United States)
Hanging (many countries)
Lethal injection (China, Guatemala, Philippines, Thailand, United States)
Shooting (death by firing squad) (many countries)
Stoning (Afghanistan, Iran)

Statistics aside, European criticism of the death penalty is no different from the criticism coming out of the United States. No matter where they live, death penalty opponents argue that the system is racist, immoral, and unjust. No matter where they live, death penalty supporters argue that the system is fair, just, and moral.

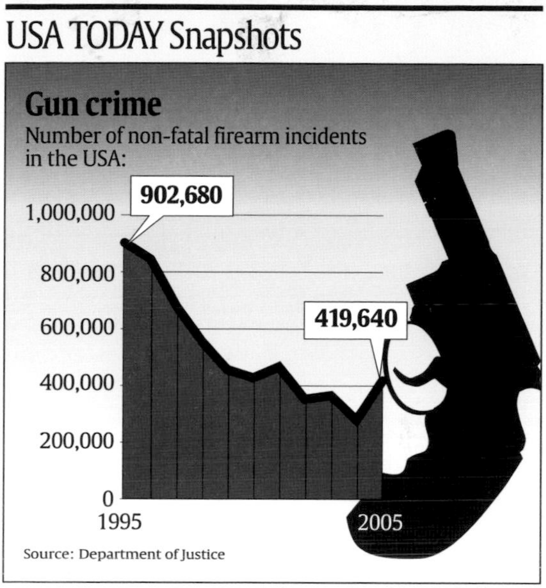

By David Stuckey and Keith Simmons, USA TODAY, 2007

EQUAL·JU

## CHAPTER ELEVEN

# Future Directions

WITH THE *GREGG V. GEORGIA* DECISION IN 1976, THE U.S. Supreme Court ruled that capital punishment does not violate the U.S. Constitution. Therefore, capital punishment is legal in the United States. It's up to each state to decide whether or not to use it.

Thirty-five states allow the death penalty, and fifteen states do not. But these numbers can change. In some non-death-penalty states, such as Minnesota, citizens have campaigned to have the death penalty reinstated. And in every state that uses the death penalty, people have organized to have the death penalty repealed.

New York State reinstated the death penalty in 1995. But in 2004, the New York Court of Appeals ruled that the death penalty violated the state's constitution,

*Left:* The U.S. Supreme Court building in Washington, D.C. The Supreme Court plays, and will continue to play, an important role in shaping death penalty policy in the United States.

thus putting New York back on the list of non–death penalty states. The New Jersey state legislature declared a moratorium on executions in that state in 2006 and officially abolished the death penalty in 2007.

New Mexico is the newest state to abolish the death penalty. The state legislature voted for and the governor approved repeal in the winter of 2009. As of March 2009, lawmakers in Colorado and Montana were also considering anti-death penalty legislation.

## NEW BLOOD ON THE HIGH COURT

When death penalty cases can't be resolved on a state level, they are often appealed to the U.S. Supreme Court. Several recent Supreme Court decisions have

*Above:* New Mexico governor Bill Richardson signs a repeal of the state's death penalty law on March 18, 2009.

placed limits on capital punishment. For instance, *Atkins v. Virginia* (2002) prohibited the death penalty for mentally retarded people. *Roper v. Simmons* (2005) banned the death penalty for those who commit crimes as juveniles (defined as aged seventeen or younger).

> **"Almost no one feels detached about capital punishment. Advocates, opponents, and those in conflict [undecided] all see in the issue a struggle for the national soul."**
>
> **—SCOTT TUROW,**
> ATTORNEY AND AUTHOR, 2003

The Court's next death penalty ruling (June 2008; *Kennedy v. Louisiana*) decided that child rape is not punishable by death. These decisions were controversial and angered many death penalty supporters. Even the Court itself was divided on all three decisions.

The Supreme Court is a changing body. The U.S. president appoints new justices to the Court to replace justices who die or retire. In late 2005, President George W. Bush appointed two new justices to the Supreme Court, Chief Justice John Roberts and Justice Samuel Alito, both well-known conservatives with pro–death penalty leanings. Commentators who follow the Court predicted that under Roberts, the Court would be more conservative than under the previous chief justice, William Rehnquist. The April 2008 *Baze v. Rees* ruling, which said that lethal injection is not cruel and unusual punishment, bore out that prediction. Yet the Court's June 2008 ruling against the death penalty for

*Above:* The U.S. Supreme Court is divided in its stance on the death penalty, and the makeup of the court is likely to change during President Barack Obama's term in office.

child rape was a more liberal position, although the most conservative justices did dissent, or express their opposition to the ruling.

## REFORM

Will the United States abolish the death penalty through federal action at some point in the future? It seems unlikely. In theory, the U.S. Congress could outlaw the death penalty. But with support for the death penalty at 64 percent in the United States, that move would be very controversial and difficult to pass into law. More likely, individual states will continue to make their own decisions about whether to preserve or abolish the death penalty, as New Mexico did when it ended the practice in 2009.

Reform of the death penalty system is also likely. In 1997 the American Bar Association (ABA), the national association for U.S. lawyers, passed a resolution urging a halt to all executions in the United States until the death penalty system could be reformed. The ABA believed that the system needed to be made fairer, with a minimum risk of executing an innocent person. In 2004 the ABA carried out a study of capital punishment in the United States, based on information from eight sample states. The study, published in 2007, found the existence of:

- Significant racial disparities in imposing the death penalty
- Judges who let a desire for reelection influence their death penalty decisions
- Inadequate representation of the mentally ill and mentally challenged in capital cases
- Fraud and mistakes in crime labs and medical examiners offices

As a result of this study, the ABA again urged a moratorium on executions until these and other problems could be remedied.

To address similar concerns in Illinois, in 2002 the Governor's Commission on Capital Punishment issued a series of recommendations for reform of that state's death penalty system. These recommendations included:

- Making DNA testing mandatory in every death penalty case
- Providing DNA testing for all inmates already serving on death row
- Enforcing higher competency standards for defense attorneys
- Punishing prosecutors who withhold relevant evidence from defense attorneys
- Taping police interrogations and suspects' confessions to prevent police brutality or the forcing of false confessions from suspects

In 2004 the Illinois state legislature passed some of the recommended reforms, but Illinois has not yet lifted the moratorium.

## DOLLARS AND CENTS

Beyond reforms, politics, and public opinion, perhaps the one factor that will determine the future of the death penalty more than any other is money. States simply can't afford the high price of keeping prisoners on death row. The California Commission on the Fair Administration of Justice estimates that the state spends $138 million per year on the death penalty and needs another $95 million per year to get the system operating properly. Because of budget shortfalls, death row prisoners in California must wait about four years before even being assigned an attorney to handle their first appeal.

The United States entered a severe economic recession in 2008. State governments have had to slash their budgets. They have had to make tough decisions about which programs to fund and which to cut. In some states, it appears that the death penalty might fall victim to budget cuts. Many states don't have adequate funds to pay for death row prisoners' defense and appeals. If the states can't come up with the money, they might have to abandon the death penalty.

USA TODAY Snapshots®

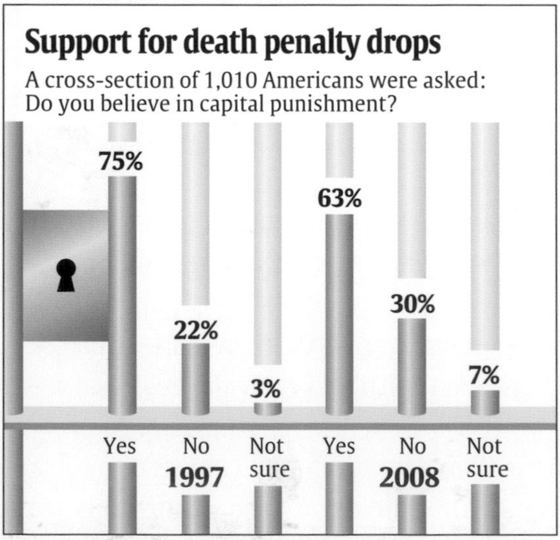


Source: HarrisInteractive By David Stuckey and Adrienne Lewis, USA TODAY, 2008

## WHAT'S NEXT?

Statistics show that the death penalty has lost some traction in the first decade of the twenty-first century. The number of new death sentences per year has declined, from a high of 328 in 1994 to just 111 in 2008. The number of executions has also fallen, from a high of 98 in 1999 down to just 37 in 2008.

The low 2008 figure has an easy explanation. For the first four months of the year, all states put executions on hold, awaiting the Supreme Court decision on lethal injection. Nevertheless, a look at the numbers shows an overall decline in executions, as follows:

| Year | Number of Executions |
|---|---|
| 1999 | 98 |
| 2000 | 85 |
| 2001 | 66 |
| 2002 | 71 |
| 2003 | 65 |
| 2004 | 59 |
| 2005 | 60 |
| 2006 | 53 |
| 2007 | 42 |
| 2008 | 37 |

What has caused the decrease? Supreme Court delays and decisions? State reforms and moratoriums? High costs? DNA exonerations? Changing public opinion? Most likely, all of these factors have influenced the trend. Will the trend continue? Will more states abolish the death penalty? Will other states reinstate it? Whatever the future holds, the death penalty is sure to remain a hot-button issue.

## TIMELINE

| | |
|---|---|
| **1700s B.C.** | Babylonians create the Code of Hammurabi. The code lists twenty-five crimes punishable by death. |
| **circa 1000 B.C.** | Writers begin creating the Hebrew Bible, which describes an "eye-for-an-eye" system of punishment. |
| **1608** | The Jamestown Colony in Virginia executes George Kendall for spying. He is the first person executed in the North American colonies. |
| **1767** | Italian scholar Cesare Beccaria argues against the death penalty. |
| **1834** | Pennsylvania passes a law banning public executions. |
| **1852** | Rhode Island becomes the first state to abolish the death penalty. (It is later reinstated there.) |
| **1863** | Venezuela is the first nation in the world to completely abolish the death penalty. |
| **1890** | New York murderer William Kemmler is the first American to die in the electric chair. |
| **1924** | Nevada carries out the first execution by gassing. The condemned man is Gee Jon, a convicted murderer. |
| **1935** | Executions in the United States reach an all-time high, with 197 people executed in one year. |
| **1966** | A poll reveals that only 42 percent of Americans support the death penalty. |
| **1967** | All fifty U.S. states stop executions while awaiting a U.S. Supreme Court ruling on the death penalty. |
| **1972** | In *Furman v. Georgia*, the Supreme Court rules that the death penalty is "cruel and unusual punishment" and that it denies people equal protection under the law. |
| **1976** | In *Gregg v. Georgia*, the Supreme Court allows executions to resume. |

| | |
|---|---|
| **1977** | Utah murderer Gary Gilmore is the first American to be executed since executions were put on hold in 1967. Scientists devise lethal injection. |
| **1982** | Texas's Charlie Brooks, convicted of murder, becomes the first American to die by lethal injection. |
| **1986** | In *Ford v. Wainwright*, the Supreme Court prohibits the execution of the insane. |
| **1996** | The film *Dead Man Walking*, about Sister Helen Prejean and her experience with Louisiana death row inmate Patrick Sonnier, is released. |
| **1999** | Ninety-eight people are put to death in the United States, a high point for executions since capital punishment resumed in 1977. |
| **2002** | In *Atkins v. Virginia*, the Supreme Court rules that executing people who are mentally retarded is cruel and unusual punishment. |
| **2003** | Illinois governor George Ryan commutes the sentences of 167 Illinois death row inmates. Instead of death, the inmates get life in prison. |
| **2005** | In *Roper v. Simmons*, the Supreme Court rules that imposing the death penalty on people who committed crimes as juveniles is cruel and unusual punishment. |
| **2008** | In *Baze v. Rees*, the Supreme Court rules that execution by lethal injection is not cruel and unusual punishment. In *Kennedy v. Louisiana*, the Supreme Court rules that child rape is not a capital crime. |
| **2009** | New Mexico abolishes that state's death penalty. |

## GLOSSARY

**abolish:** to officially put an end to something

**appeal:** a legal proceeding in which a higher court reviews the decision of a lower court

**capital crime:** a crime that is legally punishable by death

**clemency:** an act of mercy, such as a governor changing a death sentence to life in prison

**commute:** to exchange a penalty for another that is less harsh

**conviction:** the process of being found guilty of a crime in a court of law

**death row:** the part of a prison or a prison complex that houses inmates who have been sentenced to death

**deter:** to discourage or prevent someone from taking a particular action, such as committing murder

**district attorney:** an official in charge of prosecuting cases in a city, county, or other government district. Prosecutors work to prove the guilt of someone who is being tried for a crime.

**execution:** in the death penalty system, putting a person to death legally

**lethal injection:** a method of execution that uses a combination of drugs to bring about death

**LWOP:** life in prison without parole. This sentence guarantees a prisoner will be locked up for life, with no possibility of early release.

**moratorium:** an official waiting period or delay in carrying out an action or decision

**parole:** early release of a prisoner, usually as a reward for good behavior

**prosecutor:** a lawyer who represents the government in a case against an accused lawbreaker to try to prove that person's guilt

**stay of execution:** a delay of execution that is granted by a court

**unconstitutional:** in violation of the U.S. Constitution

## SOURCE NOTES


7 Lora Owens, "Stanley "Tookie" Williams," *KnowGangs.com*, November 6, 2005, http://www.knowgangs.com/blog/tookie2.htm (May 2006).

7 Leslie Fulbright, "Tears, Anger, Silence at Protesters' Candlelight Vigil; Speakers Read from Williams' Anti-Gang Children's Books," *San Francisco Chronicle*, December 13, 2005, http://www.sfgate.com/cgi-bin/article.cgi?f=/c/a/2005/12/13/MNG0GG799G1.DTL (May 2006).

9 Exodus 21:24, (New Revised Standard Version).

11 Cesare Beccaria, "Of Crimes and Punishment," *Classical Utilitarianism Website*, 2002, http://www.la.utexas.edu/research/poltheory/beccaria/delitti/delitti.c28.html (May 2006).

13 *USA Today*, "Child Rapist Escapes Death but Not Tough Justice," June 26, 2008, A10.

14 Oren Dorell and Kevin Johnson, "Executions Drop as States Debate Lethal Injection; Some See Decline as Temporary; Others Say Death Penalty Is Fading," *USA Today*, December 18, 2006, A8.

15 Alison Motluk, "Execution by Injection Far from Painless, *New Scientist*, April 14, 2005, http://www.newscientist.com/article/dn7269 (December 4, 2008).

15 "U.S. Supreme Court, Gregg v. Georgia, 428 U.S. 153 (1976," *FindLaw for Legal Professionals*, 2009, http://caselaw.lp.findlaw.com/scripts/getcase.pl?court=US&vol=428&invol=153 (March 25, 2009).

17 Joan Biskupic and Kevin Johnson, "High Court Clears Way to Restart Lethal Injections," *USA Today*, April 17, 2008, A1.

26 Joseph M. Giarratano, "The Pains of Life," In *Facing the Death Penalty*, Michael L. Radelet, ed. (Philadelphia: Temple University Press, 1989), 3.

30–31 PBS, "Death Penalty Update," *PBS.org*, July 3, 1997, http://www.pbs.org/newshour/bb/law/july97/death_penalty_7-30.html (May 2006).

31 Kevin Johnson, "Calif. Death Penalty System 'Dysfunctional,'" *USA Today*, July 1, 2008, A3.

33 CNN, "Illinois Suspends Death Penalty," *CNN.com*, January 31, 2000, http://archives.cnn.com/2000/US/01/31/illinois.executions.02/ (December 4, 2008).

36–37 Sound Portraits Productions, "Witness to an Execution," *SoundPortraits.org*, October 20, 2000, http://soundportraits.org/on-air/witness_to_an_execution/transcript.php3 (May 2006).

40 Alex Kozinski, "Tinkering with Death," in *Debating the Death Penalty: Should American Have Capital Punishment?* Hugo Bedau and Paul Cassell, eds. (Oxford: Oxford University Press, 2004), 4.

40 Exodus 21:24, (New Revised Standard Version).

40 Ibid., 14.

40 Pat Doyle, "Trial Goes on for Family of Slain Student as Gacy Still Sits on Death Row," *Minneapolis Star Tribune*, March 26, 1990, 19A.

41 Ron Word, "Top U.S. Court to Consider Appeal on Last-Minute Challenges to Injection Executions," *FindLaw*, April 24, 2006, http://news.lp.findlaw.com/ap/o/51/04-24-2006/286d001ce8e52def.html (May 2006).

41 *U.S. News & World Report*, "Many Grieving Families Seek Comfort and Closure in the Execution of the Murderer. Do They Find It?" June 17, 1997, reprinted in "The Place for Vengeance," *Pro-Death Penalty.com*, 2006 http://www.prodeathpenalty.com/vengeance.htm (May 2006).

42 Fox News Network, "Jury Recommends Life for Lee Boyd Malvo," *Foxnews.com*, December 23, 2003, http://www.foxnews.com/story/0,2933,106483,00.html (May 2006).

42 Steve Painter, "Opening Arrest Records Split Prosecutors, Media," *BTK Wichita Serial Killer*, February 8, 2006, http://btk-profiles.blogspot.com/ (May 2006).

42 Fox News Network, "BTK Killer Sentenced to Life in Prison," *U.S. World.com*, August 19, 2005, http://www.foxnews.com/story/0,2933,166072,00.html (May 2006).

43 PBS, "Death Penalty Update."

45 Buzz Bissinger, "The Famous and the Dead," *Vanity Fair*, August 1999, http://www.danielfaulkner.com/vanity.html (May 2006).

48 John D. Bessler, *Kiss of Death: America's Love Affair with the Death Penalty* (Boston: Northeastern University Press, 2003), xv.

48 Matt. 5:38–44, (New International Version).

50 Kenneth R. Overberg, "The Death Penalty: Why the Church Speaks a Counter Message," *AmericanCatholic.org*, n.d., <http://www.americancatholic.org/Newsletters/CU/ac0195.asp> (May 2006).

50 Jacqueline Blais, "To Prejean, Death Penalty System Is Guilty as Sin," *USA Today*, February 8, 2005, D4.

51 DPIC, "New Voices: Mother of September 11 Victim Opposes Death Penalty for Moussaoui, *Death Penalty Information Center*, 2006 http://www.deathpenaltyinfo.org/getcat.php?cid=10 (May 2006).

56 Edward I. Koch, "Death and Justice," *New Republic*, April 15, 1985, 13–15.

56–57 George E. Pataki, "Death Penalty Is a Deterrent," *USA Today*, March 1997, reprinted on *Pro-Death Penalty.com*, 2006, http://www.prodeathpenalty.com/Articles/Pataki.htm (May 2006).

59 Helen Prejean, *The Death of Innocents: An Eyewitness Account of Wrongful Executions* (New York: Vintage Books, 2006), 263–264.

59 Ibid.

64 Office of the Fayette Commonwealth's Attorney, "Death Penalty Debate," *Office of the Fayette Commonwealth's Attorney*, n.d., http://www.lexingtonprosecutor.com/death_penalty_debate.htm (May 2006).

64 Joshua Marquis, "For Select Few, Death Is Just," *USA Today*, December 12, 2005, A12.

65 Scott Turow, *Ultimate Punishment: A Lawyer's Reflections on Dealing with the Death Penalty* (New York: Farrar, Straus and Giroux, 2003), 49, 50.

71 Richard Willing, "Pro-Death Penalty No Longer Safe Political Weapon," *USA Today*, June 2, 2000, A4.

74 Prejean, *Death of Innocents*, 231.

74 Joan Biskupic, "Judge Rules against Federal Death Penalty," *USA Today*, July 2, 2000, A3.

75 DPIC, "Additional Innocence Information," *Death Penalty Information Center*, n.d., http://www.deathpenaltyinfo.org/article.php?scid=6&did=111 (May 2006).

75 Ibid.

75 Office of Fayette Commonwealth Attorney, "Death Penalty Debate."

75–76 Ibid.

76 Prejean, *Death of Innocents*, 241.

76 Joshua K. Marquis, "Truth and Consequences: The Penalty of Death," in *Debating the Death Penalty: Should America Have Capital Punishment*, edited by Hugo Bedau and Paul Cassell, 117–151 (Oxford: Oxford University Press, 2004), 149.

76 Ibid.

80 NCADP, "Fact Sheet: The Death Penalty and Racial Bias," *National Coalition to Abolish the Death Penalty*, n.d., http://www.ncadp.org/fact_sheet2.html (May 2006).

80 Ibid.

82 Richard C. Dieter, "The Death Penalty in Black and White: Who Lives, Who Dies, Who Decides," *National Coalition to Abolish the Death Penalty*, June 1998, http://www.deathpenaltyinfo.org/article.php?scid=45&did=539 (May 2006).

83 Ibid.

83–84 Ibid.

86 Ibid.

88 Prejean, *Death of Innocents*, 208.

89 Office of the Fayette Commonwealth Attorney, "Criminal Justice News & Views," *Office of the Fayette Commonwealth's Attorney*, n.d., http://www.lexingtonprosecutor.com/death_penalty_debate.htm (May 2006).

89 Ibid.

91 Learfield Communications, "Capital Punishment in Missouri," *MissouriDeathrow.com*, n.d., http://www.missourinet.com/CapitalPunishment/Case_notes/simmons_christ.htm (May 2006).

94 William Schulz, "Teens Do Not Earn Right to Be Executed," *USA Today*, November 12, 2002, A22.

95 ACLU, "Juveniles and the Death Penalty," *American Civil Liberties Union*, May 11, 2004, http://www.aclu.org/capital/juv/10421pub20040511.html (May 2006).

95 Charlene Hall, ed., "Amicus Brief in Simmons vs. Roper," *Pro-Death Penalty.com*, n.d., http://www.prodeathpenalty.com/Issues/JuvenileDP.htm (May 2006).

98–99 Paul Davis, "Psychiatrists Question Death for Teen Killers," *Death Penalty Information Center*, May 26, 2004, http://www.deathpenaltyinfo.org/article.php?scid=27&did=1010 (May 2006).

99 Richard Willing, "Teen Killers' Execution Weighed; Death Penalty Opponents Seek Reversal of '89 Ruling Allowing Such Sentences for Ages 16–17," *USA Today*, October 12, 2004, A3.

101 Office of the Fayette Commonwealth Attorney, "Death Penalty Debate."

106 Tony Mauro, "Time Is Running Out; Many Troubled by Ultimate Penalty," *USA Today*, May 20, 1992, A1.

107 Robert Sherril, "Death Trip: The American Way of Execution," *Nation.com*, December, 21, 2000, http://www.thenation.com/doc/20010108/sherrill/2 (May 2006).

107 Jonathan Turley, "The Punishment Fits the Times," *USA Today*, January 16, 2008, A13.

108 Guillermo X. Garcia, "Texas Starts Year at Record Pace of Executions," *USA Today*, January 21, 2000, A13.

111–112 JFA, "Death Penalty Information," *Justice for All*, n.d., http://www.jfa.net/deathpenalty.html (May 2006).

117 Joan Biskupic, "Justices Split Hairs over Death Penalty Case, *USA Today*, April 17, 2008, A7.

118 Republican Party, "Crime," *2008 Republic Platform*, 2008, http://www.gop.com/2008Platform/Crime.htm (December 9, 2008).

123 Theresa Malcolm, "Tucker's Death Affected Robertson Views," *National Catholic Reporter*, April 23, 1999, http://www.deathpenaltyreligious.org/education/perspectives/robertson.html (May 2006).

127 National Public Radio, "Justice Scalia and the Death Penalty," *NPR.org*, June 24, 2002, http://www.npr.org/templates/story/story.php?storyId=1145509 (December 11, 2008).

129 Amnesty International, "Death Penalty Developments," *Amnesty.org*, n.d., http://web.amnesty.org/pages/deathpenalty-developments2005-eng (May 2006).

129 Kevin Johnson and Guillermo X. Garcia, "Europeans Keep Vigil at Texas' Death Row," *USA Today*, December 14, 2000, A21.

137 Turow, *Ultimate Punishment*, 24.

## SELECTED BIBLIOGRAPHY

Banner, Stuart. *The Death Penalty: An American History.* Cambridge: Harvard University Press, 2002.

Bedau, Hugo. *The Death Penalty in America: Current Controversies.* Oxford: Oxford University Press, 1997.

Bedau, Hugo, and Paul Cassell, eds. *Debating the Death Penalty: Should America Have Capital Punishment.* Oxford: Oxford University Press, 2004.

Bessler, John D. *Kiss of Death: America's Love Affair with the Death Penalty.* Boston: Northeastern University Press, 2003.

Cabana, Donald. *Death at Midnight: Confessions of an Executioner.* Boston: Northeastern University Press, 1996.

Death Penalty Information Center. *The Death Penalty in 2008: Year End Report.* Washington, DC: Death Penalty Information Center, 2008.

Dow, David R., and Mark Dow, ed. *Machinery of Death: The Reality of America's Death Penalty Regime.* New York: Routledge, 2002.

Jackson, Jesse. *Legal Lynching: Racism, Injustice and the Death Penalty.* New York: Marlowe & Co., 1996.

NAACP Legal Defense and Educational Fund. *Death Row U.S.A., Winter 2008.* Washington, DC: NAACP Legal Defense and Educational Fund, 2008.

Prejean, Helen. *The Death of Innocents: An Eyewitness Account of Wrongful Executions.* New York: Vintage, 2006.

Turow, Scott. *Ultimate Punishment: A Lawyer's Reflections on Dealing with the Death Penalty.* New York: Farrar, Straus and Giroux, 2003.

## ORGANIZATIONS TO CONTACT

American Civil Liberties Union (ACLU)

125 Broad Street, 18th Floor
New York, NY 10004
212-549-2500
http://www.aclu.org

The ACLU is dedicated to preserving Americans' civil liberties: freedom of speech, association, and assembly; freedom of the press; freedom of religion; the right to equal protection under the law regardless of race, sex, religion, or national origin; the right to fair treatment in legal proceedings; and the right to privacy. The ACLU opposes the death penalty, arguing that it is applied unfairly and might lead to the execution of innocent people.

Criminal Justice Legal Foundation

P.O. Box 1199
Sacramento, CA 95812
916-446-0345
http://www.cjlf.org

The Criminal Justice Legal Foundation works to protect victims' rights and to ensure swift punishment for criminals. The foundation believes that the death penalty deters crime and is therefore committed to working to preserve its use in the United States.

Death Penalty Information Center

1101 Vermont Avenue NW, Suite 701
Washington, DC 20005
202-289-7336
http://www.deathpenaltyinfo.org

The Death Penalty Information Center provides in-depth reports, articles, statistics, and other materials on death penalty issues.

Justice For All (JFA)

9525 Katy Freeway
Houston, TX 77024
713-935-9300
http://www.jfa.net

Justice For All is dedicated to reforming the criminal justice system to better protect the lives and property of law-abiding U.S. citizens. JFA maintains a website, Pro-Death Penalty.com, with a number of articles, reports, and other information about death penalty issues.

Murder Victims' Families for Human Rights (MVFHR)

2161 Massachusetts Avenue
Cambridge, MA 02140
617-491-9600
http://www.murdervictimsfamilies.org

MVFHR is an association of family members of murder victims who oppose the death penalty. The organization argues that vengeance is not the right approach to dealing with murder and charges that the death penalty is a violation of human rights.

# FURTHER READING, WEBSITES, AND FILMS

## BOOKS

Arriens, Jan. *Welcome to Hell: Letters and Writings from Death Row.* Boston: Northeastern University Press, 1997.
This book takes readers to a place very few people ever go—death row, where more than three thousand Americans currently await execution. In their own writings, inmates offer their personal stories, including information about their lives behind bars and their impending executions.

Edge, Laura B. *Locked Up: A History of the U.S. Prison System.* Minneapolis: Twenty-First Century Books, 2009.
Since colonial times, Americans have debated how best to treat people who commit crimes. Should they be locked away to keep society safe, or should they be rehabilitated in hopes that they might someday become better citizens? This book examines these questions and changing attitudes toward criminal justice through U.S. history.

Faulkner, Maureen. *Murdered by Mumia: A Life Sentence of Loss, Pain, and Injustice.* Guilford, CT: Lyons Press, 2007.
When Mumia Abu-Jamal was sentenced to death for killing police officer Dan Faulkner in 1982, Faulkner's wife, Maureen, thought justice had been done. But more than twenty-five years later, Mumia has obtained a sort of celebrity status on death row—and the Faulkner family still awaits justice. In this book, Maureen Faulkner gives her personal views on the Abu-Jamal case.

Henningfeld, Diane Andrews. *The Death Penalty.* Farmington Hills, MI: Greenhaven Press, 2006.
This title brings together opposing viewpoints from a variety of books and other documents to examine the death penalty from all angles. Topics include Supreme Court decisions, DNA testing, and death penalty reform.

Kukathas, Uma, ed. *Death Penalty.* Farmington Hills, MI: Greenhaven Press, 2007.
This collection of essays from scholars and other experts includes both pro- and anti-death penalty arguments, with discussions about deterrence, vengeance, racial bias, juvenile murders, and other key questions.

Williams, Mary E., ed. *Is the Death Penalty Fair?* Farmington Hills, MI: Greenhaven Press, 2003.
This title brings together essays from professors, journalists, researchers, and other experts. They consider whether the death penalty discriminates against African Americans and other minorities, poor people, and the mentally ill.

## WEBSITES

Amnesty International USA
http://aiusa.org
Amnesty International is dedicated to protecting human rights and freedoms around the world. The website offers extensive information about the death penalty in the United States and around the world.

Criminal Justice Legal Foundation
http://www.cjlf.org
The Criminal Justice Legal Foundation works to protect victims' rights and to ensure swift punishment for criminals. The foundation believes that the death penalty deters crime and is therefore committed to working to preserve its use in the United States.

Death Penalty Focus
http://www.deathpenalty.org
Death penalty Focus is an anti–death penalty organization. Its website offers a host of information, including statistics, articles, and links to other websites.

Moratorium Campaign
http://www.moratorium.org
Founded by anti–death penalty activist Sister Helen Prejean, the Moratorium Campaign is fighting for all death penalty states to halt its

use, with the ultimate goal of ending the death penalty throughout the United States. The website offers extensive links to other anti–death penalty organizations and resources.

Murder Victims' Families for Human Rights
http://www.murdervictimsfamilies.org
When a family member is murdered, many people want revenge in the form of execution. Members of this anti-death-penalty organization have chosen a different way to heal their wounds. They argue that the "eye-for-an-eye" mentality only perpetuates violence and hatred in society.

Pro-Death Penalty.com
http://www.prodeathpenalty.com
Pro-death-penalty forces have far fewer Web resources than their anti-death-penalty opponents. This site is one place where those who support the death penalty can find articles, links, and other information.

## FILMS

*Deadline*. DVD. Chatsworth, CA: Home Vision, 2004.
This documentary film examines the death penalty debate, with specific focus on Illinois, where flaws in the legal system compelled the governor to empty death row in 2003.

*Dead Man Walking*. DVD. Los Angeles: MGM, 2000.
Released in movie theaters in 1996, this riveting film tells the story of a murderer awaiting execution in Louisiana. Sean Penn plays Matthew Poncelet (based on actual murderer Patrick Sonnier), while Susan Sarandon plays the real-life Sister Helen Prejean, who befriends and counsels him on death row.

*The Exonerated*. DVD. Thousand Oaks, CA: Monterey Video, 2006.
Adapted from the stage, this film dramatizes the experiences of six people sentenced to death for crimes they didn't commit and for which they were later exonerated. The script is taken in part from actual court transcripts and other legal documents, as well as inmates' own words and writings. Well-known actors (Susan Sarandon, Danny Glover, and others) portray the six inmates.

*Twelve Angry Men*. DVD. Los Angeles: MGM, 2001.
This 1957 film classic focuses on the jury in a capital murder case. Eleven jurors are convinced that the defendant is guilty. The twelfth juror, played by Henry Fonda, tries to make the case for innocence.

## INDEX

## PHOTO ACKNOWLEDGMENTS

The images in this book are used with the permission of: © David Paul Morris/Getty Images, pp. 4–5; © Hector Mata/AFP/Getty Images, p. 6; © Hulton Archive/Getty Images, pp. 8–9; The Granger Collection, New York, p. 11; © DeA Picture Library/Art Resource, NY, p. 12; Gramercy Pictures/Everett Collection, p. 16; AP Photo/Grant Halverson, pp. 22–23; AP Photo/The Charlotte Observer, Jeff Siner, p. 24; AP Photo/Tim Shaffer, p. 28; © Bo Rader/Getty Images, p. 30; © Bob Daemmrich/The Image Works, p. 34; AP Photo/Tony Gutierrez, p. 35; © Zed Nelson/Reportage/Getty Images, p. 36; AP Photo/Paul Sakuma, pp. 38–39; © Tim Dillon/USA TODAY, pp. 43, 100, 138; AP Photo, p. 45; © Nicholas Kamm/AFP/Getty Images, p. 48; © H. Darr Beiser/USA TODAY, p. 49; Rex Features USA, p. 51; AP Photo/Bill Wolf, p. 52; © iStockphoto.com/Michelle Junior, pp. 54–55; AP Photo/Tim Roske, p. 56; © J. Davenport/San Antonio Express/ZUMA Press, p. 62; AP Photo/Andy Scott, pp. 66–67; © Eileen Blass/USA TODAY, p. 69; © TEK Image/Photo Researchers, Inc., p. 70; AP Photo/Mark Wilson, p. 72; © Getty Images, pp. 78–79; AP Photo/Lou Dematteis, p. 83; AP Photo/Sam Mircovich, p. 87; AP Photo/Missouri Department of Corrections, pp. 90–91; AP Photo/Tom Gannam, p. 92; AP Photo/Elaine Thompson, pp. 102–103; © The Bakersfield Californian/ZUMA Press, pp. 110–111; © Ash Knotek/Snappers/ZUMA Press, p. 112; REUTERS/Robert Galbraith, p. 119; © Kenneth Lambert/Washington Times/ZUMA Press, p. 122; © Yoshikazu Tsuno/AFP/Getty Images, pp. 124–125; REUTERS/Max Rossi, p. 126; REUTERS, p. 128; © istockphoto.com/VisualField, pp. 134–135; AP Photo/Jane Phillips, The New Mexican, p. 136.

Front cover: © David J Sams/Stone/Getty Images.

## ABOUT THE AUTHOR

JoAnn Bren Guernsey has published three young adult novels and coauthored a mystery series dealing with environmental issues. Her published nonfiction topics include teen pregnancy, rape, missing children, animal rights, and a biography of Hillary Rodham Clinton.